adapt

adapt

DISRUPTION IS COMING
TO COMMERCIAL REAL ESTATE BROKERAGE
ARE YOU READY?

BLAINE
STRICKLAND

Adapt: Disruption is Coming to Commercial Real Estate Brokerage. Are You Ready?

Copyright © 2020 Resourceful Publishing, LLC. All Rights Reserved.

No part of this publication may be reproduced, stored in a retrieval system, or transmitted in any form or by any means—electronic, mechanical, photocopying, recording, or otherwise—without prior written permission from the publisher, except for the inclusion of brief quotations in a review.

For information about this title or to order other books and/or electronic media, contact the publisher:

Resourceful Publishing, LLC
1027 Colleton Alley, Winter Garden, FL 34787
HBS-Resources.com
Blaine@HBS-Resources.com

Library of Congress Control Number

ISBN Print: 978-0-9997690-3-4
ISBN eBook: 978-0-9997690-4-1
ISBN Audio: 978-0-9997690-5-8

Cover Design by Elena Reznikova

Interior Design by Adept Content Solutions

Printed in the United States of America

CONTENTS

PART ONE

CLIENT EVOLUTION

PART TWO

PLAYGROUND OF THE GIANTS

PART THREE

DEMOGRAPHIC EVOLUTION

This book is dedicated to
my father, Robert K. Strickland, CCIM,
and my son, Hunter R. Strickland, CCIM,
who together with me
form a three-generation family of CCIM designees.
Collectively, we represent the past, present, and future
of the commercial real estate brokerage industry.

We are as ready for disruption as you are.

PREFACE

The advice I offer in my first book, *Thrive*, was gleaned from the lessons I learned over a long career as an agent, broker, manager, and owner of commercial real estate. Many agents have commented on how the prescriptions in the book helped them accelerate their productivity.

A few agents, though, offered a different perspective.

"I'm not as concerned with my productivity today as I am with my existence tomorrow."

"The industry is changing rapidly. I wonder how long I will be relevant."

"I wish I could get some glimpse into the future. I want to be ahead of the curve."

Where *Thrive* is written as a how-to book, this book has a what-if message. How can we prepare for the future? *Adapt* explores an entirely new set of questions.

What lies ahead? Can we identify the changes that are coming and estimate their impact? How can we adapt to the reshaping of the industry?

I began to ponder these questions even before *Thrive* was published. Over the past two years, I have explored potential answers with a wide variety of players within the industry. I've attended conferences, interviewed thought leaders, read extensively, hired researchers, polled audiences, and just plain pondered.

Adapt is different from *Thrive* in two ways. First, it isn't (and can't be) based on experience. This book is my opinion about the information I've assimilated over two years of focused research. Every concept in this book could turn out to be untrue or irrelevant.

Second, this book targets a much wider audience. Where *Thrive* was aimed at producers, this book invites the consideration of everyone who touches the commercial real estate brokerage industry. Real-estate owners, property managers, investors, lenders, users, venture capitalists, academic institutions, and all the peripheral vendors who interact with commercial real estate agents will benefit from thinking about the future of those agents. Many of these allied groups will be affected by— or potentially advance—the imminent disruption of the industry. The future that I examine will affect all these stakeholders.

An overwhelming majority of the focus groups I conducted strongly agreed the pace of change over the next ten years will be significantly greater than over the last decade. What do you think? Even if I have identified only one or two factors that will cause disruption, it seems imperative that we start the discussion now.

FOREWORD

Change.

It's a word you won't often find uttered or talked about in the largest industry on earth, commercial real estate. Nonetheless, *change* is a word I am obsessed with. It has been the driving force for me personally and professionally for much of the past three decades. It guides my every decision and is my own North Star.

For many reasons, this massive industry, one that I have spent the better part of thirty-five years working in, avoids change. It is too closely associated with another word that sends shivers down the spine of most commercial real estate professionals: *risk*.

Little has changed over the years in the commercial real estate industry, especially the brokerage sector, because it really hasn't had to. Everything has worked extremely well for decades in this thriving sector. There are clients, and there is constant demand. There are owners and managers, and they understand their respective roles. There is space and there are properties. And in the middle lies the real estate professional who puts the pieces together to create a transaction that attempts to satisfy all parties. Rinse and repeat. Over and over and over again. Year after year. Decade after decade.

In an industry that adheres to the "eat what you kill" philosophy, "change" and "risk" are putting what is "proven" and "predictable" in unavoidable jeopardy. With so much at stake and when one bad decision can be fatal, why step out of your comfort zone? Especially over the past decade, which is one of the great bull runs of all time.

Everything and everyone involved in this process work to preserve the status quo as much as possible. The title agents, the marketers, the analysts, the researchers, the lawyers, the accountants, and all the way through and up and down the food chain. Predictability sustains many, many aspects of this industry.

Since 2011, I have been focused on doing everything I can to bring innovation to the world of commercial real estate. Through my company, CREtech.com, we are building a community of tech professionals that are passionate about helping this industry embrace change. We have built a sizable audience of startup founders, venture capitalists, brokers, landlords, academics, thought leaders, and many others. All are working tirelessly to embrace change and help the industry manage a period of unprecedented disruption in the economy and future-proof itself against these powerful forces. But we have so much work to do and are still such a small fragment of the industry at large.

There hasn't been an industry on earth that technology has not disrupted. Ours will not be immune, despite the beliefs of those who are so entrenched and are delusional enough to think commercial real estate is just too complex for tech to impact it. Tell that to stockbrokers in the financial services sector. Or to travel agents. Or those in the medical community, who are the next to feel it. Every professional, every industry, will be impacted by technology. The only difference is that some industries and professionals understand this and anticipate it, while others simply refuse to see it coming. And for the latter, it is often too late. Think retail brick-and-mortar real estate and the impact of e-commerce as a great example. While malls were being built, Amazon was going about shredding the traditional retail sector to pieces.

Skate to where the puck is going, not to where it has been.
—Wayne Gretzky

For me, our own Wayne Gretzky in commercial real estate is Blaine Strickland. Few people think and write about disruption in the commercial real estate industry other than Blaine. I was a fan of his first book *Thrive* even before we had connected. He is one of the few people in our industry who sees the world as it is and where it is going. The fact that he comes from commercial real estate and has been so successful in it, gives his words and ideas even more weight.

As Blaine says, "*Disruption* means 'Didn't see that coming!'" It often occurs quickly and massively. It can start slowly and build speed rapidly." Because of forces that are beyond the control of those in commercial real estate, change is coming and it's coming fast. Not one single aspect of the industry will be immune to these forces beyond our control. Everything is up for grabs. The forces of disruption are happening all around commercial real estate—the new nature of work, demographic changes, the demand for shorter-term lease options, the growth of flex-space, artificial intelligence, and so many more meaningful trends are changing the way corporations are viewing space. For the first time in my career, the customer is driving change in ways never seen before.

Tenants are demanding tools and environments that cater to their changing workforce. They want technology at their fingertips, and they demand the flexibility to respond to rapidly changing economic conditions. As a result, we are seeing new types of real estate emerge and the entire development category converge on new use types, often all in a single structure. "Space as a service." "Cities as a service." The nature of work, living, and shopping is being redefined around the world. In real time.

And as Blaine accurately says in *Adapt*, "Commercial real estate is simply not prepared for it."

The good news for those who are reading this Foreword is that what follows in this book is your blueprint for navigating change. I so often get emails and calls from my peers or have conversations at our conferences about where to begin with adopting technology. Finally, we have a road map for commercial real estate to future-proof itself against technology forces and embrace innovation. While this book is focused mostly on the broker, as they are probably the ones at the greatest risk, it applies to everyone in the industry. What is needed most in commercial real estate is a change of mindset that sees both "change" and "risk" with entirely new meaning.

The commercial real estate brokerage professional who does not change and embrace innovation is truly at risk.

Welcome to the future.

Only the paranoid survive.
—Andy Grove

Michael Beckerman
Chief Executive Officer, CRETech

INTRODUCTION

The City Council Chambers were packed. The atmosphere was tense. There were lots of suits in the room, but there were lots of protestors with matching t-shirts, too. The meeting was called to order. The mayor announced that it was the intention of the council to hear all sides regarding the issue of whether Uber and Lyft should be allowed to operate in Orlando. If so, what were the appropriate conditions to ensure rider safety—and to protect the 80-year-old local taxi firm that was a leading contributor to the community?

Discussion ensued. Cheers shouted and boos erupted. Ultimately, the City Council of Orlando unanimously approved the operating rules for Uber and Lyft in Orlando. Its approval was grudging, though: The ride-share companies had to charge higher fares than the taxi company. It was December 2014.

In May 2017, Florida's governor, Rick Scott, weighed in.

"I'm proud to sign this legislation today to make it easier for ride-sharing companies to thrive in Florida and help ensure the safety of our families," said Scott in a statement. "Florida is one of the most business-friendly states in the nation because of our efforts to reduce burdensome regulations and encourage innovation and job creation across all industries, including transportation."

In the ensuing press conference, the governor stated that Florida was a tourist state, and tourists expect to be able to use ride-sharing in

Florida—as they do across the world—for quick, safe, inexpensive transit. He told the cities and airports across Florida to figure it out; the future is now. The restraints on Uber and Lyft fares melted away. Capitalism, in the form of market demand and surge pricing, would take over.

In April 2018, the *Orlando Business Journal* reported that the taxi company had abandoned its twenty-acre site and that the land was under contract to a national REIT for industrial development. The taxi company that had grown to a fleet of 1,200 taxis and had monopolistic control over the market, and especially the linkage from Orlando International Airport to Disney World, was effectively dismantled.

Now that's *disruption*. Not reshaping, not modifying, not retooling. Disruption means "not doing it like that anymore." It is not interruption—like when a traffic accident ties up the interstate. An interruption slows or stops progress temporarily, but then the same pattern resumes.

Disruption is not simply change. We've all been amazed at the increasing speed of our mobile phones. They've gotten faster, smarter, and (in some cases) cheaper. Wireless phones, though, existed in the 1970s and will likely be around another fifty years. Mobile phones have transformed the way we communicate, but they primarily speed up something we've always done—interact with each other.

Disruption means "a whole new way." When my family moved from its home of twenty years last summer, we parted with a custom bookcase that was filled with a twenty-four-volume set of encyclopedias. The custom feature was a special slot in the bookcase for a giant atlas—a two-inch-thick book full of color maps. It had been a wedding present thirty-five years earlier. We hadn't touched those encyclopedias for many years, and the bookcase was covered with dust. Hmm. Sounds like disruption had occurred.

But disruption didn't just antiquate *my* encyclopedias. It completely fooled Microsoft. In 1993, Microsoft created *Encarta*, a multimedia, multi-language encyclopedia that was sold through downloads and

CDs. Sales were robust—and my family was a subscriber through those content-hungry years of middle school and high school.

In 2009, Microsoft abandoned *Encarta*. It had been completely replaced by an internet-based encyclopedia that was broader, deeper, constantly current—and FREE! *Wikipedia* launched in 2001 and had grown quickly due to the loyalty of its volunteers, who tirelessly edited the content for accuracy. It raced past *Encarta* as the encyclopedia of choice and today is the default information source for fact seekers across the globe. Ironically, about the only place you can learn about the long-gone *Encarta* is on *Wikipedia*.

Disruption means "Didn't see that coming!" It often occurs quickly and massively. It can start slowly and build speed rapidly. Who foresaw that within a single decade commercial banks would go from building massive lobbies on expensive downtown corners to incentivizing you to *not visit* the bank by using mobile deposits?

Several futurists, including Bill Gates, have been credited with quoting a form of Amara's Law (attributed to Roy Amara, Stanford professor, who reportedly coined the law in the 1970s) that often accompanies the observance of disruption: We overestimate the amount of change that will occur in one year and underestimate the change that will occur in five years.

Arthur C. Clarke put it this way in 1951: "If we have learned one thing from the history of invention and discovery, it is that, *in the long run—and often in the short one—the most daring prophecies seem laughably conservative.*"

Some have used the phrase *creative destruction* as a code word for disruption. The term was first coined in 1942 by Joseph Schumpeter and has been used extensively ever since. Economists usually use the term to talk about the march of capitalism and innovation, hand-in-hand, to radically change economic structure.

If you are as cool as I, you might still have a Peaches record crate at home. This small, wooden crate was sold by a popular record store for the purpose of toting your 33-rpm phonograph records back and forth to your friend's house for an afternoon of singing along and secretly practicing your *American Bandstand* moves. I distinctly remember going into a Peaches store in the early 1980s to buy new copies of my favorite records because the stores were carrying fewer records and many, many more 8-tracks and cassettes. I was afraid that my prized records might not be available anymore.

Little did I know that I would soon be buying VHS tapes and then DVDs at Peaches. Like everyone else, my strolls through Peaches would eventually be replaced by jaunts to Blockbuster and then Redbox. Finally, today, I stream music on my phone and watch movies streamed by Netflix on my flat-screen television.

Because of the "Netflix effect," we all bandy about phrases like "cutting the cord" and "subscription model" and "content aggregator" easily. My Peaches crate is just a fondly regarded relic now.

Here's another twist on the path of creative destruction: In mid-2019, Uber and the taxi company that it put out of business announced a new partnership in Orlando called UberTaxi. Uber supplies all the benefits of the app to taxi drivers, and the taxi company supplies more than 650 new drivers and vehicles. In the 72-million-annual-visitors market of Orlando, Uber could hardly keep up with demand; it needed a radical increase in capacity. The opponents became creative collaborators to the benefit of both.

—◦◦◦—

It's crucial to determine how you feel about disruption. Is it a bad thing? Do you yearn for things to stay the way they are? Or is it a good thing, as humankind evolves its potential for greater reach and understanding?

How do you feel about the creative destruction of the 125-year-old commercial real estate brokerage industry?

This is a crucial question to ponder as you read on. You may feel that I have envisioned a gloomy future for our industry because I make a case for coming changes that will be highly significant if I am right, or almost right. I explained these concepts to one focus group and then polled them for their reaction. Finally, I asked for questions and comments. Some wanted to argue the concepts. Some felt that a few forces could cause disruption that is much more powerful and imminent than others. Overall, though, there was a sense of shock—change really is coming!

I think the commercial real estate brokerage industry is on the verge of significant disruption. It appears to me that a handful of powerful forces are poised to have disruptive effect. I outline these forces in the upcoming chapters. I also give you my perspective on the implications of each force and possible ways that you can prepare (or at least watch) for them. In the "Conclusion," I'll revisit the sum effect and return to the quandary of creative destruction.

—◦◦◦—

Before we get to the nine forces I've identified, though, let's briefly consider two other sources of disruption that are absolutely part of the equation. I cover them in the "Introduction," but I won't deeply evaluate them or integrate them in the remainder of the book. These two sources will affect all of us, globally, but because they are not unique to the commercial real estate brokerage industry, I mention them here alone.

SOURCE ONE: ECONOMIC EVOLUTION

Disruption might flow merely from economic evolution.

As of this writing, most economists think we are "over our skis"—the recovery cycle has been too long by historical standards. This has been the longest recovery in the 170 years that the Federal Reserve Bank has charted our economy.

Three years ago, economists on podiums stopped answering the "What inning are we in?" question because their calibration by historical standards couldn't reckon with the US economy that wasn't cooling. Today, the few who will answer the question usually say something like, "I don't know—but it has to be extra innings."

We are coming off the Great Recession. But could this long-winded recovery (the Great Recovery?) that has succeeded the Great Recession foretell another painful fall?

It's hard to say. We are in uncertain territory. Here are the most commonly cited reasons for significant economic disruption:

Diminished Human Resources

- The composition of our workforce is changing. The giant tranche of Baby Boomers is being replaced, numerically, by Gen X and Gen Y, along with a massive influx of immigrants, almost all of whom come from Spanish-speaking countries.[1] While the population is enlarging, the body of skills is not. In Orlando, as an example, there are 300 unfilled professional engineering jobs—in the shadow of the giant University of Central Florida, which awards 1,500 engineering degrees every year. If you want to learn more about this skills gap, treat yourself to Mark Lautman's book, *When the Boomers Bail: A Community Economic Survival Guide.*

- The birth rate in the United States has dropped five years in a row and is now at its lowest point in thirty-two years. The current level of births is below the estimated rate at which generations replace themselves. Many countries in Europe have been below replacement rate for many years, which is why they are dependent on immigration for growth. The United States is at the doorstep of this same condition.

Dwindling Natural Resources

- Water is the most fundamental natural resource on the planet; we cannot live without it. Fortunately, it is not leaving the planet. Instead, it is changing conditions and locations. We have too little water in arid regions (and often in agricultural areas) and too much water in coastal communities. Battles over clean water—and its many applications—are already underway.

- The battery elements—cobalt, lithium, nickel, and copper—are also in high demand and short supply. In many cases, poor countries have these elements available for mining, and rich countries want them for their technology growth. This is a gargantuan mismatch, and the uneven pursuit of these resources across the globe creates tension. None of these battery elements qualify as the "conflict minerals" (cassiterite, wolframite, coltan, and gold) that have fueled decades of bloody conflict in the Democratic Republic of the Congo. These minerals are crucial to capacitors and other electronic device applications and are often extracted from militarized mines. Could scarcity lead to larger battles?

Blatant Trade Wars
- In 1773, the American Colonies were united because of a trade war with Great Britain, and trade wars have been part of the American experience ever since. Where we once dumped tea in the harbor to protest unfair tariffs, we now suffer rapidly changing prices on Amazon. We fight our own little trade battles every day. Collectively, these trade wars create dangerous imbalances in the import/export arena. What happens when one country effectively owns another?

- To this day, our politicians still campaign on trade-war concepts—expansionism, isolationism, nationalism, protectionism, and capitalism. When the positions harden, tension erupts. Fissures emerge—and pirates board ships and drones bomb refineries.

Massive Amount of Underserved Investment Capital
- With the onset of the "great recovery," we have seen the lowest cap rates in memory. Because of the inverse relationship between cap

rates and value, this translates to the highest prices in history. One explanation for these record-low cap rates stems from the intense competition to get the great wealth of investors deployed into assets that offer return on investment. Investors are bidding higher and higher prices in a nearly desperate attempt to capture growth.

- The risk related to these investments has not abated. Risks that were formerly priced at 7 percent are now priced at 5 percent, but the change in "reward" does not reflect the corresponding change in "risk." In other words, despite the old developer's prayer ("Lord, please just give me one more booming market, and I promise I'll be restrained this time."), we are potentially (predictably?) back at the edge of a market-warping correction. But what is an investor to do? "If I don't invest, my money will sit in cash and I will miss the opportunity for growth."

So, what is the disruption that could flow from these economic factors? Will the disruption take the same form that it has in the past? Some of my more frightening guesses look like this:

- **Faster, more violent economic swings.** It seems counterintuitive to presume that the economic needle will jerk more rapidly when we are on the heels of the longest recovery ever, which occurred after the longest recession ever. Aren't the cycles lengthening rather than shortening? Perhaps. The Federal Reserve Bank strives to keep cycles as mild as possible. But look at the history of cryptocurrency— the so-called future of money because of its non-political foundation. The value of Bitcoin increased from $429 in December 2015 to $17,000 in December 2017 (two years!) to $3,800 in December 2018. I think that qualifies as faster, more violent swings— don't you?

- **Zero-sum games break out.** We've generally been in an expanding cylinder of growth over the past 250 years, but now we're able to see limits. When there is a fixed number of people or finite amount of resources to go around, somebody wins, and somebody loses. If a country or community doesn't like the limits it sees, should it be entitled to try its hand as a "winner" against a potential "loser?" Does growth trump all other issues? What do you make of the "$10,000 offer" employed by Tulsa, Oklahoma, (and other communities in a variety of forms) to attract remote workers to the community? Is this monetary incentive the new entry fee in a zero-sum game?

- **Discipline completely erodes in the investment arena.** We're the Madoff generation—where investors continued to give funds to a money manager despite ten years of doubts by regulators. Bernie's rate of return was unprecedented, unexplained, and eventually proven to be impossible. Investors around the world wanted the story to be true. In the end, Madoff defrauded investors of $65 billion. Wow. This is what happened when investors were seduced by above-market returns; what happens if the seduction seeps down to mere average levels of return?

What could these economic conditions mean to the commercial real estate arena? It doesn't take long to conjure up horrifying images. Imagine what violent economic swings would look like to people who live primarily on commissions. Or what if default became so common that commissions were paid in arrears? (I pay commissions like I pay at a restaurant—after I'm satisfied with the meal.)

What if the zero-sum game comes to your market and it is a "loser"—no population growth, no new supply, no rent growth? Will there be any commissions to be earned in a market that is at slack tide? Maybe the slack tide will be caused by investors who can't get out—they bought at prices that haven't grown (they chased return too far) and essentially can't sell now.

But let's not go there now. Let's just leave it that all of us could be—would be—disrupted by economic factors that are broad and massive and game-changing.

SOURCE TWO: TECHNOLOGICAL EVOLUTION

Today, even teenagers know the fundamental concept of Moore's Law—that capacity and speed of computers will double every two years. We've been taught this law by Apple, who persuades us to get a new iPhone every two to three years, because, hey—who can live with 3G when 4G is up to ten times faster? Now, we are on the cusp of 5G technology, which is forty to fifty times faster than 4G LTE processors. It makes me wonder what the life of our teenagers will be like when they get to be our age.

And what about cars? We're seeing the onset of autonomous and fully electric vehicles every day. You've either ridden in a Tesla or want to. Every day, a new feature or new manufacturer or new app comes out related to the evolution of cars. It's kind of fun—maybe we will live long enough to snap our car into our briefcase like George Jetson. One futurist, Henrik Christensen of UC San Diego's Contextual Robotics Institute, predicts the opposite outcome. He believes that our kids won't even learn how to drive because they won't need to—autonomous vehicles will take them wherever they need to go. The car-that-turns-into-a-briefcase is already outdated.

On the other hand, maybe those smart kids will wish they had learned how to drive, since that's what all the astronauts will be doing soon—on Mars!

Even when we have some small toehold on technology, it is too hard to predict. Many analysts have pointed out that even if you had foreseen the explosion of personal computers in the early 1980s as they began to emerge, you would have invested your money in Radio Shack and Pet and Commodore computers. You would have been penniless by the time Apple became viable.

Today, the constant innovation flowing out of artificial intelligence, virtual reality, and hardware labs is so rapid that Moore's Law may have to be amended. We know our lives will be affected by technology, but we can't predict how—even though none of us doubts that the effect will also be massive and life-changing. These changes will affect every corner of our lives; but because of that universality, I won't attempt to identify the impact of specific technologies on the commercial real estate brokerage arena.

—◦◦◦—

So, while we acknowledge the impact of the economic and technological sources in play, let's set them aside to consider other forces that are more specific to commercial real estate brokerage. I've divided the book into three parts: Client Evolution, Playground of the Giants, and Demographic Evolution.

PART ONE: CLIENT EVOLUTION

In this section, I give thought to how our clients might evolve. They've learned to use technology and information extremely successfully in other parts of their lives, and they bring those same skills and expectations to our industry. When I started in this business, we went down to the county courthouse to look at ownership records on microfiche. Today, we expect to have a complete profile of a property pop up on our phone in a matter of seconds. It's not just instant information we expect, but also context—reviews, history, trends, and analysis are also part of the package. So far, we and the clients have evolved at about the same speed. What happens if the clients become even more powerful? Will disruption occur because the clients overwhelm us?

PART TWO: PLAYGROUND OF THE GIANTS

Sometimes, disruption occurs because there are players on the field big enough to cause it. In this section, I look at two specific players—Ten-X and Amazon—that are already in our industry and have the potential to change it radically. I also look at the large consulting firms, which are larger than our largest brokerage agencies, and ponder what moves they could make—especially since they have many of the same clients we have. Finally, I felt compelled to wonder about the future of our three largest brokerage companies: CBRE, JLL, and Cushman & Wakefield. Each of these companies is more than 100 years old and has survived multiple economic cycles, the evolution from the industrial age into the information age, and the transformation into global service organizations. What disruption would occur if one or more of our three largest players experienced a radical change?

PART THREE: DEMOGRAPHIC EVOLUTION

I was tempted to list demographic evolution as a non-specific factor. The entire country is aging, and as always, the emerging generation will bring technological innovation and cultural change. However, because our community of agents has an average age of sixty, the coming demographic shift will be much more sharply felt. The country will age gradually along an upward path; our cohort is facing a steep cliff.

Is it possible you and I will be the instruments of our own disruption? Will we still be in the industry in ten years? Because I am part of a three-generation family of CCIM designees, I think about this often. My eighty-six-year-old father is fully retired and does not play in the arena any longer. At sixty-two, I am as actively involved as ever, and (perhaps because I work out of my house) invest as many hours in my practice as I ever did. My twenty-nine-year-old son is a full-timer, actively building his career. How will that picture look in ten years? In this section, I look at the career agendas of the old guys and the new guys and find they are considerably different.

Strap in. Off we go.

PART ONE

CLIENT EVOLUTION

CHAPTER 1: **Transparency Jolts Our World**

Will commercial real estate agents experience the same disruption that happened to travel agents?

CHAPTER 2: **Access to Valuation Information Challenges an Agent's Value**

What happens when clients have easy and instant access to pricing information?

CHAPTER 3: **Onset of the Gig Economy**

Will freelancers and a buyer-controlled internet change the way we work?

CHAPTER 1

TRANSPARENCY JOLTS OUR WORLD

Will commercial real estate agents experience the same
disruption that happened to travel agents?

In the early 1980s, my wife and I decided to take in scenic New England in the fall. Our plan was to fly into Boston, drive up the coast to Ogunquit, Maine, and then make a broad arc inland through Vermont, upstate New York, and finally back to Boston for the trip home. We planned to rent a car and stay in bed-and-breakfasts along the way. We were going to be true leaf-peepers.

We contacted a friend's mother who worked as a travel agent. She loved the idea and made many valuable recommendations because she had been through that area a couple of times previously. After about a week of research and phone calls with us, she called us into her office and gave us a typewritten itinerary. She had arranged for a rental car and booked our airline flights. She had been able to make some lodging arrangements and handed us some brochures of some other places that might work. We left with a thick envelope. "I'll have the courier deliver your airline tickets about three days before you leave. I'd suggest you go over to AAA now and have them start working on your TripTik so you'll have the maps you need for your drive."

It was a wonderful trip. We took five rolls of film with us and bought at least five more. All those photographs are in an album we still look at occasionally. We kept the TripTik (check out eBay to see what these semi-customized booklets look like) for the longest time, and we still have a cookbook we acquired at one of our favorite chalets.

Sounds like a black-and-white movie, doesn't it?

It's hard to believe that the trip was crafted and executed without fax machines, cell phones, personal computers, laser printers, GPS, and the internet. By the way, I had just started my career as a sales agent at CBRE.

THE DISRUPTIVE FORCE

If you are under forty, you may not know what a travel agent is. You have never known a world without apps, websites, and TripAdvisor. Today, so much information is directly available to the traveler that involving another person would inhibit the process of making travel arrangements. The traveler can move quickly and with great certainty, and for the most part, doesn't need a travel agent. The suppliers of tickets, rooms, flights, cars, meals, and advice communicate directly with the traveler in today's world.

This open platform of communication represents the benefit of transparency. The customer can see all applicable data, presented in a usable, actionable format. Customer service representatives add to this transparency by translating details and providing comparison metrics for the customer. Allied players add context to the transparency with narrative reviews and do-it-yourself videos. Customers have learned to expect this transparency and become loyal to the most transparent vendors.

Transparency had the impact of reducing the number of travel agents from 132,000 in 1990 to 74,000 in 2014 (the last year for which I could find data). That's a 44 percent reduction in agents over twenty-four years. Some anecdotal evidence points to even fewer agents today.

What happened to those agents who left the industry? And what are the agents doing that stayed?

Many agents just departed. As information became more readily available to the traveler, they simply were not able to add value, and they moved on to other pastures.

The agents who remained in the industry adapted to the new conditions. One travel agency launched an airline. Another bought a resort. Others bought boats and buses and train cars and became part of the experience economy. Some moved into corporate planning, and some specialized in narrow niches. A few, like the agent who helps my eighty-six-year-old father with his arrangements, provide essentially the same services—although with a few gentle insertions of technology.

Here are many other readily available examples of the disruptive nature of transparency:

- **Hospitality**: You can book a week-long stay in a hotel and never interact, in person, with a member of the hotel staff. You book your room and meals and massage online. You check in online and your phone becomes your key. You can communicate any issues through the app or TV in the room. Best of all, you get a text message from the manager telling you how much they appreciate your visit, and that your points have been credited to your account. This is all "level one" transparency—your interaction with your chosen hotel.

  Prior to arriving, you engaged in "level two" transparency. You researched several hotels and narrowed your choices based on a variety of reviews. You gamed the system and forced the hotel auction site to be limited to your chosen candidates. You were rewarded with the lowest possible price for your desired choice. Then, just to top it off, you compared the hotel stay to the option of renting someone's home. You considered a wide variety of units—houses, condominiums, timeshares, and even a vintage Airstream.

If someone told you today that they were going to get a bachelor's degree in hospitality, you might be tempted to ask why. Few industries have undergone as many transformations as the hospitality industry. Maybe that's why you need a degree—to manage relentless change.

- **Online legal services:** Want to work on your will this afternoon? Need to buy some real estate? Plan to create a power of attorney for your elderly grandmother? No sweat. You'll find a template and instructions online, and you can do a credible job of acting as your own attorney. If you are a little fuzzy, you can just go to YouTube for some expert input. Hey, look at this—you can prepare your own will in ninety seconds!

  Even if you need a live attorney, you can access a human online or by phone via your prepaid legal service app supplied as part of your payroll deduction. A wide range of situations is covered by these legal services. Now you've got real representation, and you're getting the service quicker and cheaper. It must be working—customers spent $5 billion in fees for online legal services in 2017.

- **Online stock trading:** I was telling a lunch companion about a company I was working with, and how I admired its management style. He asked me a few questions, pulled up his phone, tapped a few buttons, and bought 100 shares of its stock while we were sitting there.

  "Uh," I said, "I don't know anything about their stock. I did not just make a recommendation."

  "I know. I checked them out. They have a BUY recommendation from three analysts that I follow, and their year-over-year growth looks good. Don't worry, buddy, I'm not holding you responsible."

  Just like that. It's no wonder that the number of broker-dealers registered with the SEC declined from 5,892 in March 2007 to 3,989 in March 2017. This is a 30 percent reduction in force, and the trend continues today.

In the commercial real estate arena, a new level of transparency is just now evolving. Because of the change in the FASB regulations related to operating lease reporting, a tremendous amount of data related to lease values and rates is now open to public scrutiny. Prior to this change in regulation, a company under the auspices of GAAP reporting simply consolidated data about its lease obligations and summarized it in a few statements in the footnotes. Now, much more detail is required—companies are posting numbers in the balance sheet and offering expanded narrative explanation about their real estate. Landlords, lenders, and other allies can know much more about a company's use-of-space profile than ever before.

THE IMPLICATION

The widespread transparency of valuable data in the commercial real estate arena is already a fact. Anyone can subscribe to Reonomy, CoStar, or Real Capital Analytics—constantly updated aggregations of massive amounts of specific information related to people, properties, and markets. A user or investor can come to the table now as well-informed as the agent and opposing party. The prospective buyer has seen fly-through videos of the property, scrutinized the floorplan or site plan, evaluated the ownership history of the property, examined the credit-card sales within the trade area, checked the hazardous material logs, built a spreadsheet of the sale prices of comparable properties, received an online quote for the property insurance, mapped the traffic patterns, and looked at the credit ratings of the tenants—all before the first meeting!

How much more transparency can the customer stand?

I often hear agents respond to this scenario by saying something to the effect of, "True, but we supply context and relationships and negotiation skills that are not transparent." I agree with this sentiment, if it really is true—hard-working agents *can* provide these crucial elements, and they earn every penny of their commission. Agents often have insights into market data and regulatory matters that are not easily gleaned by online research. The value of these skills is further underscored in complex transactions, where the property or the people or the market is complicated.

On the other hand, many commercial transactions are not as complex. Single-tenant, net-lease properties often trade quickly and with very little surrounding conversation because they are commodity-like in their evaluation. These properties tend to be straightforward in their analysis and highly comparable to other similar properties, and they trade in a narrow band of pricing. The simpler the transaction becomes, the more eligible it is for trading without the involvement of an agent.

> **If customers perceive that they have enough information to act without the assistance of an agent, and that acting alone saves them money, they are highly likely to act.**

Let's keep in mind, also, that it is customers' perception that matters most in this discussion. If customers perceive that they have enough information to act without the assistance of an agent, and that acting alone saves them money, they are highly likely to act.

What kind of disruption will occur in the commercial real estate brokerage arena as a result of all this transparency, especially since it feels so like the other examples we've noted?

Three of the most significant implications are:

1. **Fewer agents overall:**
   - Many agents will simply fall by the wayside. These are the agents who have few personal relationships and are dependent on sign calls, brochures, and mass mailings. These are the agents most easily replaced by transparency. Customers can obtain the same information quicker from online sources. That information is

likely to be more comprehensive, more transferable, and more contextualized than receiving a two-page flyer from the agent.

o Some compression will be due to the increased productivity of their peers. If a brokerage team maintains strong relationships and masters the applicable technology, they are likely to conduct more transactions per agent than they have in the past. In other words, some agents will do more deals—which potentially takes those deals away from the marginal providers.

2. **Lower commissions and/or flat fees:**
   o If customers can perform most services themselves, will they expect a lower fee to be charged? I remember trading stocks early in my career by calling my stockbroker. He executed my trade, called me back, and mailed me a confirmation letter. On my monthly statement, I could see that I paid a commission equal to 2 percent of the purchase price. If I made a $10,000 trade, I paid a $200 commission. Today, I make that trade myself on my phone, get instant confirmation, and pay $7 for the trade. I could move to another trading platform that is offering free trades. Is this our future?
   o Perhaps the menu of services will be segmented. Because some of the information or services are available directly to the customer, agents may choose to offer services on an *a la carte* basis. As an example, a client might say, "I've already received proposals from three landlords. I need your help in negotiating with them. I'd be willing to pay $300 an hour for your time."

3. **A changing scope of services:**
   o As I've morphed from being a classroom instructor to teaching more online and blended-format courses, I've been exposed to this mantra: You'll be moving from a sage on the stage to a guide on the side. In other words, you no longer control the

learning process; you enable students to learn and help them enhance their own learning methods. In the brokerage arena, this might translate to helping prospects find additional information or translating the information they've assembled.

o In an upcoming chapter, I discuss the implications of the value proposition offered by the Ten-X auction platform. For the moment, consider that Ten-X installs an agent on every property it brings to auction. However, its expectations of that agent center entirely on enabling the potential buyers to act decisively. In other words, they expect the agent to field all questions, conduct tours, ensure compliance with the process, and help the buyers justify a price above the reserve. Ten-X doesn't need help with outreach, or qualifying buyers, or structuring the deal; it needs a cheerleader.

There could be other implications related to transparency. What if commercial agents become subject to the same rating system that HomeLight has built for residential real estate agents? It claims to have analyzed 27,000,000 transactions and has ratings on over 2,000,000 agents. The ratings are instantly viewable on the app. Moreover, the rating system itself has earned hundreds of 5-star ratings by its users.

What would it feel like to be rated by your clients? How does transparency feel now?

If all these implications turned out to be real, it would be fair to say that transparency changed our scope, our fees, the size of our fraternity and even the way we are hired. That's a serious jolt.

ARE YOU READY?

Here are some ideas you could pursue if you perceive that increased transparency is coming to your world.

- There's a story about a man who came to America from the Old World and brought his considerable woodworking tools with him. He soon realized he could make and sell wooden buckets to the townspeople, and over the years, his mastery caused a small business to blossom. When the man's son took over the business, he expanded the distribution to a wider market, and the business grew even larger. Finally, after nearly fifty years in business, the third generation took over. Sales increased for a while but then started to decline rapidly. When the grandfather and father met with the grandson to try to understand why the business was failing, they stressed that their wooden buckets were universally admired and worth every penny of their forty-dollar price tag. In their opinion, the grandson should be able to maintain, if not grow, the business as they had done.

  "Why have people stopped buying our wooden buckets? We have the best buckets in the business!"

  "That's true, grandfather," said the grandson. "The problem is that we are not in the wooden bucket business any longer. We are in the 'water carrier' business, and people can buy a plastic bucket at the hardware store for ninety-nine cents that has the same utility as our buckets."

  To paraphrase Peter Drucker, if you are not sure what business you are in, just ask your customers. They will tell you. Exactly what business are you in?

- Enhance your own value proposition. Make time, this month, to sit down and refine your value proposition. Come up with succinct, clear-cut benefits you offer to your clients. Strive to be surefooted in the way you describe and deliver your services to clients. Think in terms of cost and efficiency. I know how powerful this exercise can be—many of my clients undertake this challenge at least twice a year.

If you are not sure where to start, try asking this question: Why do the clients we serve use brokers? What benefits do the clients seek? To what extent do our services match their needs?

- To be fair, the travel agent industry has already redefined itself. It is less than half the size it was thirty years ago, but the survivors (who now call themselves advisors, consultants, counselors, and even designers) are thriving in a world where the online world has become overwhelming to their clients. A recent Forbes article[2] about a convention for the top-end travel agents explained how far they've come in redefining their service platforms. What would "redefining your platform" mean to you?

- Monitor the savviness of your customers—are they becoming more self-sufficient? Try this: Make a list of your top (or most recent) twenty-five clients. Assign each one of them a "tech-savvy" score based on their use of technology, their ability to navigate online information, even the youth of their decision-making team. You can choose the appropriate criteria and its relative weight. Come up with an average score for the group. Take that list out a year from now, and regrade the participants. Is transparency more evident among your clients?

- Try out a "menu approach" on an appropriate client. Would he or she be willing to buy a specific service from you? Maybe the service will be a subset of what you already do—like performing a survey of available options. Or perhaps it will be a new service—like abstracting the leases of their five locations so that all the information is one place.

CHAPTER 2

ACCESS TO VALUATION INFORMATION CHALLENGES AN AGENT'S VALUE

What happens when clients have easy and
instant access to pricing information?

As pre-class homework, I asked my group of undergraduate real estate students to go to the Zillow website and read the small print about "Zestimates," which are the estimates of value produced by their proprietary algorithm. This was Zillow's explanation of how it considers several elements of comparison to come up with an approximate value for single-family homes.

In class, we walked through the methodology of the "direct sales comparison" approach to value in an appraisal and contemplated the confidence interval (the approximate accuracy) of a Zestimate. Through the process, the students gained a relatively strong grasp of the automated valuation process. As they became more familiar with how an appraisal works, they became increasingly comfortable with the values proposed by Zillow.

Then I asked them to use the Zillow app on their phone to look up the value of the home they grew up in.

The students were stunned.

Even though they knew how Zillow worked (and they trust most of the information they get from their phone every day), they couldn't stop talking about the prices they now saw in front of them. They immediately began to think about the impact of this value on their parents. For the first time ever, many had a glimpse into the wealth of their family. Some immediately exclaimed, "They should sell!"

I asked them to look at the range of values in their neighborhood and then post a few explanatory sentences on the discussion board about their conclusions. "Try to express what is happening in this neighborhood, and then offer an opinion about why it is happening," I instructed.

It was clear that the ability to see the values of a whole set of properties (their neighborhood), and its implications for a specific property within that set (their house), at the same time was a powerful exercise.

THE DISRUPTIVE FORCE

Arbitrage is the ability to capitalize on the difference between the price you pay and the price for which you sell. In the capital markets, arbitrage is often captured instantly because the two transactions occur simultaneously. Imagine buying a stock on a domestic exchange at a low price and selling it moments later on a foreign exchange at a higher price—the trade occurs quickly, and the player captures profit with minimal risk.

The only way arbitrage can occur is when a player is closely attuned to values. The player carefully watches several signals and senses when a gap occurs. This is the same exercise the students had undertaken: "Watch the big picture and the small picture simultaneously." It sounds like a low-risk proposition, but it usually requires acute, hard-earned knowledge to seize the decisive moment.

You could argue that real estate investment rarely produces a true arbitrage opportunity. Occasionally, we'll see the holder of a contract to buy real estate then sell that contract (not the real estate itself) for a profit on the same day. Or maybe you've heard the boasting of a house flipper who claims he made $25,000 in two weeks. More frequently, though, the profit between buy and sell prices takes longer to play out. For the purposes of this chapter, we'll use the arbitrage label but be more tolerant of the time and risk issue.

Because of information sources like Zillow and its competitors, arbitrage has come to the residential real estate world in a big way. These firms have scrubbed and analyzed incredible amounts of data and produced highly reliable valuations using computerized linear regression models.

The proof that this system of producing automated values is compelling has been underscored in the past few years. While some valuation platforms remain in their original form as advertising channels (the information on the app is free to consumers and advertisers pay to be in front of all those eyeballs), other platforms now use those automated values to make offers and buy homes. Zillow, Offerpad, and Opendoor have closed on billions of dollars of residential transactions. Their value proposition to sellers is straightforward: a fair price and a quick closing. In markets like Phoenix, Las Vegas, Denver, and Atlanta, the die is already cast. Recently, Zillow announced that it would be active in several more markets, supported by investors who continue to buy stock in the company and others like it.

Obviously, these firms have extreme confidence in the value estimates they create for any given single-family home. They further minimize their risk by buying many homes in the same market and creating a diversified portfolio. They know the value on a particular property may be slightly off; but, taken as a whole, they know they are protected from any small miscalculation. They benefit from looking at the big picture and the small picture at the same time.

But what does this have to do with us, the commercial real estate brokers?

THE IMPLICATION

The buyers who use automated values have disrupted the residential real estate markets in which they operate. Sellers can now contact the buying entity directly—they don't need an agent to price the property, conduct showings, and find a buyer. They make their own decisions about whether to make a repair and when to close.

The automated approach to valuation is comparatively easy to implement in the residential real estate arena. In most subdivisions, the houses are similar. They've been built by one or two contractors, they are on similar-size lots, they were built at the same time using the same materials, and they have generally similar features. This similarity enables an algorithm to predict value much more accurately.

Now, the first stage in automated appraisals is appearing on the commercial real estate horizon. Even though commercial properties are more dissimilar than residential real estate, some commercial properties (like multifamily complexes and single-tenant retail stores) are potentially eligible for the automated approach.

- Bowery Valuation, launched in 2015, has raised $19 million from a variety of venture capitalists and industry players to embed technology into the commercial valuation process. Cushman & Wakefield is an early investor and is now using Bowery's tools to enhance its own valuation processes.

- GeoPhy, a Dutch company formed in 2014, has raised $33 million for the same mission. Its founders claim the necessary information is available but hasn't been properly aggregated. It is using data from many sources, including aerial photography, to hone its valuation processes.

- Skyline AI calls itself the "artificial intelligence investment manager for commercial real estate," having "built a multidisciplinary team combining experts from the fields of data science, software engineering, and real estate." The basic premise is to use artificial intelligence to scour the blossoming amount of data about commercial real estate to find new metrics, with the intent of predicting future sales prices. The small firm raised $18 million in mid-2018 from a pool of investors including JLL.

- Groceryanchored.com is a recently-founded research company that focuses on a single asset class—neighborhood shopping centers that have a grocery store as its anchor. The investor interest in these properties is so strong that the company has been able to sell subscriptions to its constantly updated data. The founder told me they are gaining insights into this arena that have never existed before—like the seasonality of sale prices. Imagine knowing what day of the year to put the property on the market to achieve the highest sale price!

> Perhaps the application of advanced mathematical tools will have a beneficial effect on valuations—the consideration of more data might produce more accuracy.

The complexity of commercial real estate ensures that automated valuation will take longer to evolve than has been the case in residential real estate. It seems probable that the indicated prices produced by the computer-driven calculations will have a wider range. Perhaps the application of advanced mathematical tools will have a beneficial effect on valuations—the consideration of more data might produce more accuracy.

For the moment, we can begin to ponder the same questions that are being asked every day in the residential real estate arena:

- What happens when the buyer—any buyer—knows how much the property is worth before an agent is consulted?

- Does a seller perceive that pricing the property for sale is a major component of a listing broker's value?

- Is the broker's value reduced by the onset of automated valuations?

- Will an entity emerge that uses automated valuations to then make "agent-less" acquisitions of billions of dollars of commercial real estate?

The onset of easier access to a property's value is a trend to watch. If it plays out in the commercial arena in a fashion like the residential arena, we might encounter a significant challenge to the value of our services.

ARE YOU READY?

Here are some ideas you could pursue if you perceive that automated valuations are coming to your world.

- Monitor the activities of the big aggregators. Read the articles about Zillow, Opendoor, and Offerpad. If they are not in your city yet, they will be—and they are already in a nearby urban market. Are the sellers using these services? Are the agents being squeezed out?

- Have lunch with your favorite commercial real estate appraiser. You'll find that many appraisal firms are being condensed into a handful of large firms. This aggregation may make it easier to transform the valuation process—technology could be spread much quicker if everyone is under the same roof. How does your appraiser see life these days? Are his or her institutional clients eager to have quicker valuations at a lower price?

- In this vein, wander over to your municipal property appraiser office. In central Florida, as an example, the Orange County Property Appraiser's office has made significant enhancements to its database that are readily available on the public website. Although the property appraiser's job is to manage the *assessed* values of properties for the purposes of taxation, the OCPA supplies extensive *market* value information and a methodology for sifting the information. Perhaps the automated values for commercial real estate will bubble up through the public stakeholders instead of the private investors.

- Contemplate your reliance on commodity-like properties. The more easily your property can be inserted into a regression analysis, the quicker a predictive algorithm will arrive. If you broker these types of properties, you may be the first to feel the impact of automated valuation. On the other hand, you may be able to lead the onset of artificial intelligence because your database contains many insights that have not been harvested before. Your ability to manipulate the data you've collected might be the competitive edge that will catapult you past your competitors. Maybe your best action would be to slide over to Lynda.com or Khan Academy and take an introductory (and free!) course on regression analysis and forecasting.

CHAPTER 3

THE ONSET OF THE GIG ECONOMY

*Will freelancers and a buyer-controlled
internet change the way we work?*

Because I had written about the use of Gantt charts in ***Thrive***, the client in front of me wanted to know how to get started.

"I like the idea of becoming a more serious project manager, Blaine, and I would like to present a Gantt chart to my client. But I have absolutely no idea how to get started. What should I do?"

We took a few minutes to sketch out the message he wanted to convey to the client using his Gantt chart. There were about forty steps in his list of tasks to successfully navigate the representation of a tenant who wanted to change locations. These steps played out over nine months in his scheme.

"Perfect. Now, you've got the necessary ingredients to start working on your Gantt chart."

"But who is going to create the Gantt chart for me? Do you expect me to stop my world and go to project manager boot camp?"

"No. You don't have to, and you shouldn't be spending your time on this part of the process. There are millions of highly qualified freelancers already assembled for this kind of task." Welcome to the gig economy.

We opened the client's laptop, opened a free account at Upwork, and posted a detailed job listing from the concepts we had just masterminded. We specifically asked for a Gantt chart that could be presented to a layman—minimizing the details and emphasizing the big picture. Twenty-four hours later, the client had twenty bids to complete the work. The hourly rates ranged from $25 to $65 per hour, and most bidders estimated less than three hours to complete the task. Several bidders were certified in Microsoft Project (generally regarded as the gold standard in Gantt-chart creation), and two bidders were in his same city, offering to come to the client's office to meet in person. We picked out a few bidders that seemed to best fit the job, looked at the star ratings from past clients, considered the type of work they had done in the past, and selected our freelancer.

One day later, the first draft of the Gantt chart arrived by email; and three days later the Gantt chart was in final form. After ordering the Gantt chart, the client had spent about an hour providing edits and revisions through the process. The final product was "a thing of beauty" in the eyes of the client. All for $140.

Upwork claims to have 5,000,000 registered users who post about 3,000,000 jobs per year. Those jobs are responded to by 12,000,000 certified freelancers. The completed jobs have an annual value of about $1 billion. There are several other viable freelancer websites. The gig economy—where independent contractors take on short-term assignments—is in full bloom.

THE DISRUPTIVE FORCE

There are clear signs that some marketplaces are heavily influenced by the gig economy. Perhaps you've used Upwork or TaskRabbit or

Craigslist Jobs to post a task you would like someone to perform for you. Typically, you'll receive many bids and can usually accomplish your goals in an efficient and cost-effective manner.

How could the gig economy work in the commercial real estate arena?

Imagine a website where a tenant posted its need for space. The posting included size, location, suggested floor plan, timing, duration, parking requirements, signage needs, and desired budget. Once posted, the new opportunity was pushed out to a community of landlords and their brokerage representatives. The recipients of the push notice were instructed to respond by a specific date, using a specific response template, and were given a contact email address for more information.

I can hear the skeptics now: What about tenants who are just shopping, or developing evidence with which to negotiate a renewal with their current landlord? Or, what about landlords who create an imaginary tenant just to find out what the competitive landscape looks like for their own vacant space? Sure, these scenarios could happen—just like they do now in the RFP world as we currently conduct it. These are challenges to resolve, but they do not invalidate the concept.

I'm familiar with a start-up company that is striving for critical mass in this exact website scenario. Users can specify if they are lessees or buyers and input a wide range of desired characteristics. Registered landlords and agents receive notices of new listings and can search among any posted listings. The site works—deals have been identified and completed, thanks to this commercial real estate website.

Despite achieving proof of concept, it has been a rocky road for this small start-up. To make the system work, they must achieve critical mass of both users and agents. Enough respondents (agents) are needed to ensure high-quality responses to the job posters (users). Enough users (job posters) are needed to make the service worthwhile for the agents (responders). This is the essence of Metcalf's Law.[3] This company has also experimented with some allied ideas—like maintenance and property management tasks, and simply selling leads. Perhaps this start-up will close its doors, but it may have generated a road map for a larger company to pursue.

Some skeptics might also point to the investment sale arena where buyers can post their specifications for properties they would like to buy—and note that it isn't producing significant results. I'm not sure this is a fair criticism of the idea. There is so much underserved capital that buyers are using every available option to look for opportunities, including calling agents, calling landlords, and making unsolicited offers. Posting desires on a website is just another arrow in the quiver.

I could make the case that the parties in a buyer-posting portal are not equally motivated—buyers may want to buy, but sellers could be much less motivated to sell. (The presence of many applicable buyer postings may persuade a seller to hold out since his property is apparently quite desirable.) The parties are not magnetized to the portal; the buyer may have much greater desire than the seller. On the other hand, in a leasing scenario, users need space to keep their business in operation; and landlords almost always want to fill vacant space. Both parties are eager to have the portal produce results.

—◦◦◦—

There is a completely different way to imagine the impact of the gig economy on commercial real estate. What if commercial real estate agents were to become the freelancers? What if users of commercial real estate services could shop for experts on specific segments of our service offerings?

Whoops. Already happened. As of this writing, here's what the results on Upwork look like:

Phrase I used to search for freelancers	Number of freelancers who match the keywords	Range of hourly rates	Number of similar jobs posted in the past week
Real estate lease abstract	15	$15–$150	50
GIS mapping	155	$19–$150	More than 100
Negotiate a commercial real estate lease	11	$45–$375	61
Prepare an offering memorandum	4	$50–$170	5
Retail market analysis	175	$15–$400	93

Most of the freelancers are not commercial real estate agents, but several are. Almost all the potential respondents mention "commercial real estate" in the list of applicable skills and projects. Some of the respondents could easily be better at the jobs than we are—what if the lease abstract was performed by an experienced attorney? What if the mapping of location data was performed by an ArcGIS certified specialist who works at a research university? What if the retail market analysis was performed by the former head of real estate for a 100-unit chain-store firm?

It is fair to say that the gig economy has already wedged itself into our world.

THE IMPLICATION

The participants in the gig economy agree that a portal like Upwork increases speed and efficiency, reduces friction, and enhances buyer satisfaction. A gig-economy portal that really worked in the commercial real estate arena would have these same effects. Imagine a world in which users routinely and accurately posted their needs on a website. Commercial real estate agents would:

- Find prospects more quickly and could concentrate their efforts on known prospects.

- Spend less time on cold calling and sifting through suspects.

- Spend less money on creating mass marketing materials (the shotgun approach).

- Have a greater sense of the marketability of their offered space. Imagine the meeting with the landlord when you could show them the quantity and quality of applicable requests for space by prospective tenants. Or, conversely, imagine the conversation after losing out: "Here's why we lost—there were many competitors for the same tenant."

If I were a landlord, I'd find a lot to like in this list. Even if I were an agent, the efficiency and lower cost would appeal to me. Given that these commercial real estate portals have already achieved proof of concept and are starting to mature, isn't it just a matter of time before the specific and valuable benefits will soon completely overwhelm the inertia of doing it the old way?

Alternatively, if the agents become the freelancers, will they morph from commissioned salespeople to hourly paid consultants?

Alternatively, if the agents become the freelancers, will they morph from commissioned salespeople to hourly paid consultants? Would an agent go from splitting a commission with the house to keeping the entire fee inside his independent consulting company? Or perhaps the agent would mix these roles, acting as a commissioned salesperson in a specific market *and* simultaneously freelancing as an advisor on a national basis.

Is this the "escape route" that will be used by agents crowded out of the field by transparency?

ARE YOU READY?

Here are some ideas you could pursue if you perceive that the gig economy is coming to your world.

- Perhaps one of the deepest thinkers about the internet is David "Doc" Searls. Doc first began imagining the potential of the internet in the early 1990s and has since become a fellow at the Center for Information Technology & Society (CITS) at the University of California, Santa Barbara, and is a past fellow of the Berkman Center for Internet & Society at Harvard University.[4] He has been one of the clearest voices for open-source software (a collaborative approach in which licensees can distribute, improve, and extend the base program; think Linux or Firefox). Searls has also advanced the thinking about marketplaces and how the internet creates and affects them.

  In 2012, Searls published *The Intention Economy: When Customers Take Charge.* In this book, Searls makes the case for a buyer-controlled marketplace—as opposed to the vendor-controlled marketplace that now exists.

  You can find *The Intention Economy* on Amazon in a variety of formats. You can also view several explanatory videos on YouTube. You can follow Searls on Twitter and subscribe to his blog.[5]

- Consider trying out Upwork. There is some task in your world that could be done remotely. Post a task, work through the selection and execution process. Leave a rating for your freelancer. When you are done, evaluate the "guest experience." Could this same experience come to your corner of the commercial real estate world? How would it work?

- If you are really itching to experience the gig economy, perhaps you could register as a freelancer at Upwork (upwork.com). Figure out a service you could provide on an hourly basis, create a profile, and watch the job board. Bid on a job. When you win, do a good job for the client. By the way—the service doesn't have to be in commercial real estate. You can get a sense of the experience if you are a sketch artist, Instagram junkie, or someone who can translate Russian into English.

PART TWO

PLAYGROUND OF THE GIANTS

CHAPTER 4

HERE COME THE CONSULTING FIRMS

Giant, smart, capable consultancies already have
deep relationships with our clients.

As I rambled around the career resource center at a prestigious south-
ern university, it was hard not to be impressed. Today was Day
One of the recruiting season, and representatives from many large and
well-known companies were wandering the halls. Most of the people
around me—students, staff and corporate types—seemed to know the
drill. The business school had a reputation for turning out high-quality
students, and the recruiters knew their way around from past visits. The
students didn't seem to be uncomfortable; they were well trained for
this event by the staff, and they knew the ropes from their predecessors.

You could hear trendy lingo from the venture capital arena tossed
around easily. Students were asking about opportunities to pursue multiple disciplines, and recruiters wanted to know about the impact of
studying abroad. It was heady stuff.

"We're here to find the best and the brightest. We think we have an
outstanding career path to offer. We believe we are distinctive among

our industry peers. Hopefully, we'll attract the talent we are seeking," summarized one recruiter.

Wow. These companies were on their game. Most of them were consulting firms. None of the large, commercial real estate brokerage houses were represented.

Who's winning the battle for the brightest students from the best universities?

THE DISRUPTIVE FORCE

After a century as a tax and audit-oriented accounting firm, Arthur Andersen realized in the mid-1980s that its clients wanted consulting services related to allied aspects of their businesses, particularly in the information technology realm. Eventually, the consulting side of the house became bigger than the "traditional" side; and after some painful internal negotiations, Andersen Consulting split from its parent in 2000. Accenture became the name of the new consulting company.

Accenture has been a success story ever since. It earned $39.6 billion in fees in 2018. Sadly, Arthur Andersen collapsed in 2002 shortly after the Accenture departure. It's alleged role in the Enron debacle sank the firm quickly.

As it sought to increase its menu of services, Accenture eventually turned its attention to the commercial real estate issues of its clients. The primary focus of the real estate department has been property owners, and they tuck this focus into their banking channel. If you peruse Accenture's "commercial real estate asset services capabilities" web page, though, you'll find fun facts like these:

- 90,000 professionals, averaging twenty years of tenure in the commercial real estate space

- Managing more than 350,000 leases in seventy languages

- Forty percent average operational savings caused by [Accenture's] recommendations

Accenture is joined in the commercial real estate arena by the consulting practices of the remaining traditional accounting giants: KPMG, Ernst & Young, PricewaterhouseCoopers, and Deloitte. The so-called "Big Three" consulting firms—McKinsey, Bain & Company, and Boston Consulting Group—also have commercial real estate divisions. Veterans of the large brokerage houses are scattered across the leadership ranks of these units. Most of these commercial real estate units publish newsletters and hold conferences, and all promote their expertise and proven results. Each has an impressive list of clients that are the same clients served by the traditional brokerage companies like CBRE, JLL, and Cushman & Wakefield.

In 2018, CBRE ranked as the largest commercial brokerage firm, earning $21.3 billion in gross revenues. Using gross revenue as the metric, these consulting firms range from about half the size of CBRE to approximately double the size. To be fair, the consulting firms did not earn all their revenues in the commercial real estate arena like CBRE did, but it is accurate to say that the consulting firms are viable competitors in the services sector.

THE IMPLICATION

I interviewed leaders from both sides of the question: real estate consulting units and brokerage companies. How do they feel about this giant Venn diagram (overlapping circles) in which they have a large swath of the same clients?

The consensus is that the brokerage companies earn almost all the transactional fees (commissions). The consulting companies earn most of the strategy-related consulting fees. Many times, the assignments are sequential: McKinsey helps you formulate a strategy to reposition your stores, and JLL executes that strategy. McKinsey charges a consulting fee and JLL earns a commission on each transaction. These two companies serve the same client in different ways with different fee structures.

It can get interesting, though. Both sides acknowledged competing with the other on certain types of assignments. One consultant summarized it this way:

> We probably compete with the brokerage houses on about twenty assignments per year (in my slice of the market). We tend to win when the client wants a highly detailed, research-oriented result. We charge a full rate, and we still win. We often win because the brokerage company offers to undertake the assignment "for free" as part of an agreement to earn related commissions. Many times, the client views this as an add-on and may perceive it to be less important to the brokerage house than the transactions down the line. They hire us because they want a fully-vetted, non-distracted report.

It can also get complicated. The consulting companies are highly regulated and must rigorously avoid conflicts of interest. The large brokerage companies routinely control both sides of the deal and usually try to invoke the idea of a "wall" that separates the agent representing the tenant and the agent representing the landlord. These parties have opposite goals: the tenant wants the lowest lease cost, and the landlord wants the greatest lease cost. Somewhat perversely, both agents get paid based on the amount the tenant pays, raising the question of whether the agent representing the tenant is completely aligned with the tenant's interests. To further muddy the water, the brokerage firms routinely offer a rebate of their earned fees to the corporate client in order to gain control of all the client's transactional business; this is a common tactic in competition with the other brokerage houses. The laws in the many states that insist on a fiduciary relationship (complete loyalty) between an agent and his client also allow that agent to shift to a "transaction broker," who collects a commission but does not have a fiduciary relationship with either side.

This series of opportunities for potential conflict of interest is not attractive to the consulting firms. One consulting company leader pointed out that the squadron of major consulting firms would suffer if a member of the squadron failed. "Most large corporations employ multiple consultants so that they continuously have disparate parties advising them. The clients themselves must have a constant flow of feedback from non-related parties. They cannot afford any oversight that seems too friendly."

The largest battleground for the consulting firms and brokerage houses appears to be the arena of "global corporate services." These are the fee-based advisory services provided to clients who have operations around the world. Both competitors want to expand this portion of their business—so they compete for new clients and try to upsell existing clients. The brokerage firms are acutely interested in these recurring fees because they smooth out the revenue patterns of commission income that tend to rise and fall with the economy.

> The largest battleground for the consulting firms and brokerage houses appears to be the arena of "global corporate services."

CBRE blossomed to its current size over the past fifteen years by winning the "corporate services" battle over its two closest competitors, JLL and Cushman & Wakefield. In 2015, CBRE purchased Global Workplace Solutions, the facilities management arm of Johnson Controls, for $1.475 billion. Because of this acquisition and others, CBRE has a footprint equal to (or larger than) the consulting companies in terms of geography, industries served, expertise, and technology. The stage seems set for more competition in this arena.

Perhaps it will be a non-event. KPMG has battled a variety of negative events in recent years and recently paid a huge fine for bad behavior. It might be weakened to the point where it subsides or disappears. (It may not be KPMG; the sudden evaporation of Arthur Andersen less than twenty years ago shows that it could be any of the large firms.) CBRE might be the best option for a company that needs outsourced expertise and doesn't want to buy it from one of the consultancies. Maybe the disruption will take the form of CBRE's doubling in size as it takes up the slack created by a gaping hole.

Perhaps the disruption will be much more subtle than a battle for client-services accounts. What about the fact that the consulting firms are siphoning off the best and brightest at an early age? Is it likely that the talent edge on the consulting side will eventually compound to where the corporate clients perceive greater value from the consulting firms?

ARE YOU READY?

Here are some ideas you could pursue if you perceive that the consulting firms are coming to your world.

- Find and socialize the commercial real estate people within the giant consulting firms in your market. Observe their products, people, and culture. Someday you may be working with them or for them.

- Pay attention to the information the consultants produce. You won't be able to read all their commercial real estate publications, but you may pick up early warning signals. Attend their forecast events and gauge the interest from the other attendees. Why is the consulting firm holding the conference? Who is their target audience—corporate clients? Media? Talent?

- Watch closely for the firms the giants acquire. Set up Google Alerts for these companies and take note of the size of the transactions. One consulting firm leader estimated that his firm had purchased about two dozen consultancies in the past three years. Hmm. Does the consolidation on that side of the fence have any implications on the brokerage side of the fence?

- Find a way to become a part of "recruiting day" at a university that offers graduate degrees in real estate. Take note of the other firms that are recruiting the students. What is their value proposition? How appealing to the candidates is that value proposition, in comparison to yours?

CHAPTER 5

THE TEN-X COMMERCIAL EFFECT

Online auctions for commercial real estate
are a reality. Where does that leave us?

In the summer of 2012, I squeezed into a small conference room with two agents in a regional investment sales firm. The younger agent sat in front of the computer screen and had control of the keyboard. The older agent leaned over his shoulder. The auction was about to begin.

Three weeks earlier, I had toured the property with the younger agent. It was a small neighborhood shopping center on the outside edge of a small suburb. From my perspective, it was far from a trophy, but it was not a complete dog, either.

The purpose of our visit to the property was to make sure that all was well. The agent wanted to confirm that the tenants were open and operating as they had been forty-five days earlier, when he had first supplied information to the company which is now known as Ten-X. He also wanted to make sure there were no property management issues with trash or broken glass or overflowing dumpsters. All systems were go.

In short order, a couple of potential investors arrived for their separate appointments with the agent. I listened in. They were well-informed and asked appropriate questions. Both inquired about the level of inter-est from other prospective buyers, and the agent asked both, pointedly, whether they intended to make bids on the day of the auction. As we left the property, the agent was optimistic about the success of the auction.

"The reserve price is right at the valuation we gave the owner. I don't think it will be a frenzy, but we've had a lot of views on the website, and direct interaction with more than twenty possible buyers," he said.

Back in the conference room, the younger agent pointed to several visible metrics on the computer screen, including that at least forty-five buyers were online, watching the auction. When the bell rang, noth-ing happened. Finally, about thirty minutes in, a bidder made an offer about 20 percent below the strike price. Five more bids came in during the next ten minutes. With twenty minutes left to go in the two-hour window, two bidders exceeded the strike price.

"Bingo!" exclaimed the senior agent.

THE DISRUPTIVE FORCE

I had never seen an auction of non-distressed commercial real estate before. I have seen auctions of personal property, reclaimed farm equipment, excess lots in a failed residential subdivision, and the sale of tax deeds on the courthouse steps. I knew that lenders occasion-ally created a pseudo-auction—a sealed-bid process for real estate owned (REO) properties they badly wanted to eliminate from their portfolio.

As the Great Recession wreaked its destruction on the commercial real estate industry in the early 2010s, a new player emerged—the spe-cial servicers. As lenders and mortgage funds took ownership of prop-erties with defaulted financing, the special servicers were tasked with liquidating the properties as quickly as possible. "We are here to sell it by the pound," one servicer told me and showed me long spreadsheets to reinforce his point.

The commercial real estate auction was born. It wasn't really born; it was just revived on an e-commerce platform that had never existed before. I was skeptical though—commercial properties are too different from each other. Each one presents different challenges. The due diligence process takes too long. There is no way to bring the potential buyers to bear in an efficient process, I thought.

In 2017, Ten-X LLC, the parent company to both residential and commercial real estate auction sites, was purchased by the private equity firm Thomas H. Lee Partners for the equivalent of $1.6 billion. Fast forward to 2018. Here are the highlights of their performance in the commercial real estate sector to date.

- Since its launch in 2009, Ten-X has closed more than 6,200 commercial real estate deals.

- Ten-X currently has 450,000 buyers registered to bid. In order to bid, an investor must provide updated proof of funds every ninety days, and even then, is restricted to bidding on deals they can afford. At any given time, about 4,000 investors are active.

- $20 billion of commercial real estate has been transacted, cumulatively, since inception, including a $96-million sale in 2015.

- Every sale includes a broker. Ten-X has closed deals with every major brokerage house and has paid commissions to 5,000 commercial agents over its lifetime.

- The company supports a robust app. Smart devices are used to generate 30 percent of bids.

- The company holds a commercial real estate auction about every two weeks. The auctions last two days each.

- Approximately forty to fifty properties are brought to market in each auction. About half of the properties are controlled by special servicers and lenders. The other half are held by private owners who are not typically in distress.

- About 70 percent of the properties in each auction sell. The company closes about 400 deals per year. The distressed properties sell more often than the private owner properties.

Hmm. I guess commercial real estate can be effectively auctioned.

Today, Ten-X is a completely viable sales channel for commercial real estate. The argument is over. If you listened in as a Ten-X sales rep presents the value proposition to a seller, I think it would sound something like this:

- The whole process from list to auction to close takes less than ninety days.

- We enable you to know the specific date of the auction. If the property is purchased at auction, it will close in thirty days. Re-trading by the buyer happens less than 5 percent of the time.

- You can watch the auction and know exactly how many buyers are tuned in. You can see the bidding unfold.

- We can reach out in an effective and time-sensitive manner to qualified buyers. Our system enables the buyers to find your property very quickly, and then register to view the vault of stored information.

They can view the information online or via their smart devices. You can know how many buyers are making the effort to scrutinize the property.

- We work with brokers on every deal. We enable the broker to leverage technology (more information, quicker delivery, more transparency) and focus their efforts on the interested buyers.

- We will work with you and your agent to set the price. Our huge database of completed deals gives us the ability to predict the price buyers will pay. We allow you, within limits, to set the starting bid and the reserve price.

Sounds compelling—and it is. Tune in to an auction and see for yourself. Go to the Ten-X website, create an account, choose a property that interests you, and look for the auction date for that property. When the auction occurs, you'll be able to see what has happened. If you want to watch the live bidding, you'll have to register to bid.

THE IMPLICATION

In the focus groups I conducted in preparation for writing this book, Ten-X was a lively topic. Agents in some markets were only vaguely aware of Ten-X. Other markets rated them as the single most impactful force for disruption over the next decade. Only a few agents had closed a deal with Ten-X, but most of them knew of at least one property that had been taken to auction. In every audience, several agents voiced concern.

So why the angst? Many factors emerged in these discussions.

- When Ten-X really gained traction as the market recovered in 2011–2014, the special servicers turned to Ten-X in force because the auctions were working. The servicers had lots of real estate to dispose of, and the auctions were helping them offload it effectively (because buyers were coming back in to the market). At that time, Ten-X seemed to be indifferent to the brokerage companies. It seemingly broadcast the message, "We don't need you." Even though the company has consistently worked with brokers since inception, some mistrust still lingers.

- Ten-X is very efficient. Every property goes through the same process, and every transaction occurs using the same documents. The sales occur on a designated date. The buyers all squeeze through the same portal. Some agents take advantage of those benefits and frequently encourage their sellers to use the auction methodology. Other agents fear this efficiency and wonder if they are feeding their looming competitor by bringing their clients to Ten-X.

> Ten-X is very efficient. Every property goes through the same process, and every transaction occurs using the same documents.

- Because Ten-X has amassed a huge database of sales data (imagine the data mining that must be occurring when every sale closes online), some agents fear the company will eventually displace them. A Ten-X agent could easily say to a seller, "here are the sales of the last twenty-five properties most like yours. You should expect to sell it in this range." This feels like the beginning of the end to some agents. One agent predicted that Ten-X will hire agents as salaried representatives as it grows. When it has a highly functioning database and a slew of salaried agents, wouldn't Ten-X be self-sufficient? Couldn't they change their policy of installing a broker in every listing?

- Some agents simply fear what feels like imminent explosion. Google was an early-stage investor in Ten-X in 2014. Given that Google has $100 billion in cash stashed over at headquarters, will they reinvest? Or will they perhaps push their friends over at eBay (quite experienced auctioneers who have already tiptoed into real estate transactions) to get involved? Ten-X sold for "only" $1.6 billion two years ago and has continued to prove its viability. Isn't it ripe for acquisition by a like-minded partner?

Let's keep this in perspective. CBRE sold about $80 billion of commercial real estate in 2018; Ten-X has sold $20 billion over the last 10 years. Isn't Ten-X just a distant competitor?

You might think that. But the agents I asked don't. The streamlined nature of their process, the data they collect, and the speed of their ascension puts them squarely on the list of potentially disruptive forces.

Keep in mind that the disruption will flow from the auction of commercial real estate, not the company. Like the earliest makers of personal computers, Ten-X may go out of business. The bigger issue is the durability and evolution of this sales process.

ARE YOU READY?

Here are some ideas you could pursue if you perceive that the Ten-X effect is coming to your world.

- Spend fifteen minutes on the Ten-X website. It's informative. Try to look at it through the lens of a prospective seller. Is it compelling? When you observe the properties listed for sale on Ten-X, is it intriguing to you? Would the properties you sell fit into the Ten-X profile?

- Ask institutional sellers or local commercial bankers about their experience with auctions in general and Ten-X in particular. Are they ever "sell by the pound" sellers? In what conditions do they start to care more about certainty of process than sale price?

- Find the Ten-X representative for your region. Find out how it works, and what your next steps might be. Ask how you get on the list of appointed brokers (those agents who are appointed by Ten-X when a seller comes to them directly). What would their expectations be of you, the agent, in those situations?

- Give it a go. List and sell a property on Ten-X. You'll be much better at gauging the potential disruption after you have walked through the process with a real deal.

CHAPTER 6

THE AMAZON EFFECT

The elephant in the room is already stomping around in our world.

"Good news! Your neighborhood is now part of Amazon Prime Now," exclaimed the postcard.

I read the details and decided to use the $10 off coupon for my first order. Eighty-seven minutes later, the contact lens solution, batteries, and copy paper I ordered showed up at my door. I glanced past the delivery-man and saw a minivan with a small Amazon sign on the door. Wow. The fantasy of my orders being delivered by drone in thirty minutes (already in business as Amazon Prime Air) suddenly seemed a whole lot less futuristic.

We've all marveled as Amazon has changed our lives. I was ecstatic in the old days when I could just search their massive library and order almost any *book*. You click the order button and it arrives in the mail! Amazing!

Now, we count on Amazon for almost every *product*. More people use the Amazon search engine to look for products than Google. We count on Amazon for online music, movies, and reading material. Amazon powers my doorbell, and Alexa updates me on news almost every morning. Of course, I pay an annual fee to be part of the Prime tribe. I'm so happy with their performance that I am OK with Jeff Bezos becoming the richest person on the planet—and remaining so even after his divorce.

It's been a fascinating journey of twenty-five years for all of us Amazonians.

THE DISRUPTIVE FORCE

Scott Galloway, an NYU professor and author of *The Four: The Hidden DNA of Amazon, Apple, Facebook, and Google*, says we ain't seen nothin' yet.

Galloway has made an extensive study of the four most influential companies in the world: Amazon, Google, Facebook, and Apple. He notes that if the gross revenues of these four companies were combined, that sum would make them the seventh-largest *country* in the world.

He's contemplated the products and services they sell and the way their customers react to them. He's examined their growth, their acquisitions, their interactions with regulators, and their leadership. Ultimately, Galloway has come to this conclusion: Amazon will be the grand prize winner. It already outpaces the other three, and it will eventually destroy (or consume) them because it has trod into their territory and does what they do better than they do it.

What, then, does this mean to the commercial real estate arena?

Consider these Amazon story lines as a commercial real estate player:

- Amazon is one of the largest users, if not *the* largest, of commercial real estate space in the world. In their EOY 2018 Form 10-K, Amazon reports that it leases over 270 million square feet of office, retail, and industrial space and owns another 11 million square feet across the globe, for a total of 281 million square feet. Almost 200 million square feet of this space is in the United States.

- When Amazon acquired Whole Foods in August 2017 for $13.7 billion, it acquired 500 stores (and a network of distribution warehouses) across the US. It has already started to merge those store locations with other Amazon functions like Amazon Locker and Amazon Prime Now. Notably, the stock prices of Whole Foods' competitors plunged on the day of the acquisition.

- When Amazon acquired a defunct mall in northeast Ohio, it quickly turned it into a fulfillment center. It enlarged the usable space, created new jobs, increased the tax base of the community, and gained a formidable puzzle piece in its last-mile strategy. Most nearby residents are happy about the transformation of the derelict property and generally look past the claim that Amazon probably put the mall out of business in the first place.

- In mid-2017, Amazon announced that it would be expanding from its headquarters in Seattle and was immediately undertaking a search for a location that could house 50,000 employees. Amazon created a request for proposal for its "HQ2," and 238 cities across the US entered the beauty pageant. The prize was so compelling that the cities aggregated data about themselves that had never been assembled before. From a site-selection viewpoint, it was the greatest commercial real estate exercise in history. Cities now know more about themselves than they ever would have known without going through the process. Who holds all that data? Amazon. If you thought Amazon was a powerful negotiator as the largest user in the country, how powerful are they when they are also the most knowledgeable?

> If you thought Amazon was a powerful negotiator as the largest user in the country, how powerful are they when they are also the most knowledgeable?

You might make the case that Amazon is, first and foremost, a commercial real estate behemoth—and, oh yeah, it sells a bunch of stuff, too. This "multi-headed hydra" is so massive and so impactful that every move is a disruption of some kind.

THE IMPLICATION

It's hard to know where to start if you are contemplating the implications of Amazon's forays into commercial real estate. It is tempting to leave it at this: When Amazon sneezes, we all catch cold. We don't know if they are going to sneeze, shiver, hiccup, yawn, or just scratch their nose. We do know they are relentless. (They still own their original URL—relentless.com.) When they so much as blink, it will have an impact on commercial real estate.

But let's take a shot at some possible implications:

- Amazon has its hands on a lot of commercial real estate. They could easily assemble a real estate company just to manage their own properties. Would this company be a property management company? Would this company offer third-party services akin to Amazon Web Services (AWS—the company that sells Amazon's data analytics and cloud storage *to its competitors*)? Would it take the form of a real estate investment trust (REIT)—offering investors the opportunity to own Amazon's real estate?

- Amazon has a lot of employees and hungers for more. Would Amazon create a residential real estate company just to manage the housing needs of its employees? Would it buy Zillow so that it could buy homes in the markets where it locates its people and profit from the increase in values? Maybe it will just tiptoe into residential real estate like it has with its partnership with Realogy—offering

Amazon gift cards to homebuyers that use a Realogy (Century 21, Coldwell Banker, ERA, and others) sales agent.

- Will Jeff Bezos take on the real estate forays himself? He's already the twenty-eighth largest landowner in the country. Maybe he'll create a city near Florida's Cape Canaveral where he controls 300 acres for his Blue Origin space venture. Or perhaps he'll create the city on the 30,000 acres he owns in Texas. What real estate will he control in Arlington, Virginia, or Nashville, Tennessee, the two big winners, so far, in the HQ2 sweepstakes?

Amazon has about $40 billion of cash on hand and a fearless attitude about new ventures. Maybe its biggest impact will flow from some new project that hasn't even been conceived yet.

In the focus groups I conducted prior to writing this book, every respondent knew something about Amazon, and they weren't surprised when they learned a new tidbit in the group exercises. The Amazon effect was consistently named as the most probable cause of disruption in the commercial real estate brokerage arena. Now, if we could just figure out what the disruption will look like.

> The Amazon effect was consistently named as the most probable cause of disruption in the commercial real estate brokerage arena.

ARE YOU READY?

Here are some ideas you could pursue if you perceive that the Amazon effect will disrupt your world.

- Treat yourself to Scott Galloway's book, *The Four: The Hidden DNA of Amazon, Apple, Facebook, and Google*. Galloway does an admirable job of making his case. He's all over YouTube and TEDx, too, so you can listen to his conclusions if you don't want to read them. One of the more concerning conclusions relates to the way the Big Four respond to government regulation. Be sure to pick up on his comical explanation of how the Whole Foods acquisition went down.

- Jeff Bezos has been protective of his personal background. To learn more about him, read *The Everything Store* by Brad Stone. It's a comprehensive look at both the family background and corporate evolution of Bezos. The author tracked down many of the early executives of Amazon and was finally given insider access to the Bezos family. Stone is a pro, and the story is well told. You might take a moment to read some of the reviews of the book on Amazon; many are thoughtful analyses of some small turn in the story.

- Want to see Amazon in action? You can take a tour of an Amazon fulfillment center. These are million-square-foot temples of technology. There are about seventy-five existing fulfillment centers in North America, and Amazon currently offers tours in twenty-three of them. You can make your reservation online.[6] If you can't make the journey, there are a handful of videos, including a short one from Amazon, that will give you a sense of what it is like to be inside a whirring, whistling building equal to the size of twenty-five football fields.

- You could make a lifetime study of the HQ2 exercise. To grasp the enormity of the information that was produced, start by checking out the first-tier request for proposal issued by Amazon.[7]

  You can read numerous explanatory articles about how communities responded (Tucson dragged a twenty-one-foot-tall saguaro cactus to Seattle) and how Amazon began to sift through the materials. You can also search for the actual submission made by your community—or any other. You'll be amazed at the production quality of the responses. You can search directly for the proposal from your city, or just search for "HQ2." You'll get 686 search results[8]; as you scroll down, you'll find the proposal you are seeking.

- I recently heard an industrial real estate insider say this: "Amazon is our largest tenant across our very large portfolio. As this relationship has grown, we've learned that everyone, and I mean everyone, must have an Amazon strategy. Municipal planners, contractors, property owners, and managers—even adjacent tenants—must have an Amazon strategy." This caused me to pause, again, and think about my personal strategy for simply selling books on Amazon. Am I maximizing the almost limitless reach of Amazon? Are you?

- If pondering the future as shaped by Amazon is just too much, and you need an adult beverage, consider finding a Whole Foods store that is accompanied by an Amazon Locker location.

Here's the story one millennial told me:

I buy a lot of stuff, including clothing, from Amazon. I live in an apartment, but I don't have my purchases delivered there. I have them sent to the Amazon Locker that is on my way home from work. I just stop by and pick it up. (Don't tell anyone, but I often buy two or three sizes of the same item and try them on in the bathroom. I just return the 'wrong' sizes right on the spot by putting them back in the return locker.) Because the Amazon Locker is at the front door of Whole Foods, I go into the craft-beer bar—it used to be just the coffee bar, but they expanded it and now offer beer, wine, and food—and meet my friends. We usually listen to the musician for a while, then grab something for dinner and head home.

I checked it out for myself. It is true—the Whole Foods café, with its crowd spilling out on to the patio, is the place to be. What better way to ponder disruption?

CHAPTER 7

THE CRAFT BEER EFFECT

Perhaps the largest brokerages will grow in a new way in the future.

I saw the Uber driver's eyebrow arch when I confirmed I was going to the Moxy Hotel in Tempe.

"How did you find out about the Moxy?" he asked.

"My client told me it was the new, cool place to stay."

"It is that. I think you'll *probably* like it."

I knew what he was getting at—Moxy was developed by Marriott for the millennial crowd, and I seemed slightly outside the target market. But the location was perfect and the price was right, so I decided to give it a go.

As I walked in past the pinball machines and was greeted by the fully tatted, nose-ring-wearing bartender, she asked me if I was checking in.

"Yes. Where is the front desk?"

"Right here. I'll check you in and get you a beer."

After dropping my stuff in my room (and, admittedly, playing an Elvis record on the phonograph), I came back down to the lobby for that beer. The bartender/front desk clerk explained my choices, and I selected a locally brewed IPA that was outstanding. As I snuggled into a beanbag chair, it occurred to me that Marriott was competing in a whole new way. This was a long stretch from the buttoned-down image they cultivated for so many years. I knew they had significantly expanded their portfolio of brands by both acquisition and development. I queried Marriott brands on my iPad and discovered that there are now thirty brands that range from super luxury to however you would describe the ultra-hip Moxy. Although the market segmentation is wide, there is one powerful commonality: All the brands award Marriott Rewards points. Hmm. A controlled competition of sorts.

A few minutes later, I searched for more information about the beer I was drinking and stumbled upon an August 2018 article in the *Chicago Tribune*: "Anheuser-Busch on its way to becoming king of craft beer too." The writer detailed the unsuccessful efforts of Anheuser-Busch to create its own craft beers, and its realization that it could buy small craft breweries and accelerate them by infusing its resources, starting with its unrivaled distribution network. Anheuser-Busch has now bought ten craft breweries across the country, and when the grocery/big box store sales of those beers are aggregated, they can claim to be a top seller of craft beer. The writer notes a claim by some analysts that because of the rebel nature of the craft brewing community, drinkers would not buy as much of those craft beers if they knew Anheuser-Busch was the parent company.

Interesting. Marriott is a long way from the Ritz, and Anheuser-Busch is a long way from Budweiser. These two giants in their respective industries have evolved in game-changing ways. As I started the second beer, I began to ponder the growth strategies of the giant firms in our industry.

THE DISRUPTIVE FORCE

Let's take a moment to define the giants. Here are the most recent details about the three biggest players in the commercial real estate brokerage arena.

Firm	2018 Gross Revenue	Approximate Valuation	Number of Associates
CBRE	$21.3 billion	$20.2 billion	90,000
JLL	$16.3 billion	$8.8 billion	90,000
Cushman & Wakefield	$8.2 billion	$4.2 billion	51,000

Source: https://craft.co/cbre-group/competitors. All three companies are public; data drawn from SEC reports.

Observations: All three companies are headquartered in the US but provide services across the globe. The services provided by each company are generally like the others—brokerage, capital markets, appraisal, project management, and property management. A quick glance at the office locations of each firm reveals that the companies have about 85 percent overlap in service areas.

Conclusions: The Big Three firms are similar to each other, but CBRE is the largest player when judged by revenues and valuation.

I tried to develop an order of magnitude in terms of the sales-agent (not total personnel) count in the three giants versus the whole industry. I made several informal attempts. I asked insiders for their estimate of the agent count in each organization. I also counted all the agents on the rosters of the Big Three in five cities and compared them to the total number of commercial agents registered with LoopNet in the same city. The best guess I could come up with is that about 8 percent of all full-time commercial agents in the US are associated with one of the Big Three firms.

I estimate that this 8 percent of the total domestic commercial real estate brokerage population probably accounts for at least 50 percent of the dollar value of commissions earned. My estimate is anchored by the guess that the Big Three control 80 percent of the corporate, multi-market transactions and about 20 percent of the local street brokerage. Many of the agents associated with the Big Three firms are annually recognized as the top producers in their markets. Simultaneously, there are many agents who identify themselves as commercial agents with smaller firms but produce very little commission income in the commercial arena. It's a guess, I admit. What do you think the ratio is in your market?

For the moment, play along with me: If the Big Three control 8 percent of the people and 50 percent of the commissions, what are their growth strategies for the next ten years?

Over the *past* ten years, the central figure in this discussion was Brett White. He joined CBRE in 1984 in the San Diego office but was running the company's brokerage services division by 1998. By 2005, White was the company's CEO; and by 2011, he had acquired the Trammell Crow Company and ING. He led the company into its pursuit of corporate services work and significantly ramped up the revenues of the company. In 2012, in his early fifties, White stepped down (perhaps involuntarily) from CBRE to enjoy more time with his family. By all accounts, he was a relentless pursuer of growth opportunities in his twenty-eight years with CBRE, and he extended the company's hold on the #1 spot on the list of largest commercial brokers.

In 2014, White suddenly reappeared on the scene—this time as the chairman of DTZ, a global-but-smaller commercial real estate firm based in Chicago. In short order, DTZ acquired Cassidy & Turley for $557 million, and then Cushman & Wakefield for $2.04 billion. DTZ changed its name to Cushman & Wakefield, and White continues to serve as the Chairman/CEO of the company today.

The man who captained CBRE through a massive growth stage from 2005–2012 is now in charge of the third-largest firm. He's made many public comments about building Cushman & Wakefield into a competitor for the top spot. He's young enough, and he has the incentive, skill, experience, and capital to be the dominant player in the arena for the *next* ten years as well.[9]

Will Brett White be at the center of the coming disruption caused by the actions of the Big Three? Possibly. Some insiders feel there is a lot of heavy lifting to be done to enlarge Cushman & Wakefield to the revenue levels of CBRE and JLL. Cushman & Wakefield was not as enterprising as the other two in the era before White's arrival, and it must work hard to double in size if it wants to compete for the top spot.

THE IMPLICATION

Each of the three biggest firms continues to seek opportunities to grow through expanded corporate services, global reach, and acquisition.

There has also been a noticeable effort to capture each other's top producers. Agents in every major US city can point to top producers in one of the Big Three firms moving to one of the other two over the past two to three years, usually with a large signing bonus in hand.

Perhaps the implication for disruption is that the Big Three will simply intensify their current growth strategies: more acquisition, more locations, more cannibalization. Maybe it will work—ten years from now, the Big Three will account for, say, 20 percent of the people and 75 percent of the gross revenues in the commercial real estate brokerage arena. If this occurs, the disruption will be obvious: the players on the rosters will shift continuously, and the market will constantly have to readjust to new names and faces.

On the other hand, maybe a craft-beer strategy will kick in. In this scenario, one of the Big Three buys a local, high-quality firm and does not absorb it. Instead, like Anheuser-Busch, it just infuses it with resources: access to global markets, IT infrastructure, subject-matter expertise, and long-standing relationships. The big boy doesn't try to change the culture of the little boy; it may even understate or hide its investment. Or, taking a page from Marriott, it lists all its brands under the same banner, acknowledging the different segments served by each brand.

When Anheuser-Busch acquired the five-year-old, Asheville-based Wicked Weed craft brewery in mid-2017, it bought a local brewer most famous for its sour beers sold from its popular Funk House. You don't have to work hard to imagine what a stretch that must have been for some conformists at Anheuser-Busch, and how quickly the brand would have died if they had insisted on "Bud-Lighting" its new acquisition. Instead, Anheuser-Busch now has a front-row seat in the Best Beer City in the USA, according to Serious Eats.

Most of us know a small, local commercial real estate brokerage firm that is unlikely to agree to be acquired by a giant. They love their culture, and their clients are long-standing and loyal. They dominate their niche. They are like a chef-driven, artisanal restaurant—they have only twenty-four seats, but you must make reservations a month in advance, and three months for Valentine's Day. The chef would never be willing to be acquired by Darden Restaurants.

Maybe Brett White and his peers will take a page from Marriott and Anheuser-Busch, both holders of large market shares who then turned their efforts on quiet, effective market segmentation. That would be interesting to watch, wouldn't it?

As warming as that vision might feel, we should think about a completely different potential disruption. Think back over the chapters about the consulting firms and Amazon. Ponder these questions:

- PricewaterhouseCoopers is about three times larger than CBRE in people and twice as large in revenues. It is a private company and carries little debt. It has significant cash. PwC uses agents from each of the Big Three firms to execute its own real estate transactions, so it knows how commercial real estate brokerage works. Because there is a significant overlap in clients served, is it conceivable that it would purchase CBRE to simply expand its own corporate service platform? Most insiders frowned on this possibility due to the heavy regulatory burden on the big accounting companies. They warmed to the idea, though, that segments of CBRE's business (and a few of their key leaders) could be interesting to PwC.

- Amazon currently owns or leases approximately 281 million square feet of commercial real estate across the globe. We've already pondered if it should form a company to manage its real estate. If it purchased CBRE for its current valuation near $20 billion to manage, lease, build-out, and finance all that space, the acquisition would equate to just over 2 percent of Amazon's value. Would Amazon benefit by self-supplying services to its real estate portfolio?

- What if Google, who was an early investor in Ten-X, beat Amazon to the punch? CBRE represents about 5 percent of Google's valuation. Google doesn't control as many square feet as Amazon, but much of it is in California, where CBRE has a massive footprint. And, just for fun, what if Google also decided to buy CoStar (a global commercial real estate information provider—tech company—currently valued at $17 billion) at the same time, just to make sure the CBRE acquisition had that dominant feel Google loves?

- Perhaps CBRE and its top two competitors are undervalued as enterprise companies. What if a private-equity pirate bought one of these companies and sold it for its parts? What would the list of buyers look like if you could buy just the property management portfolio, or just the valuation unit, or just the corporate services component?

We must look at the future of the Big Three to adequately consider disruption. They've had a long, stable run in their current configuration. Perhaps that will continue. Perhaps disruption will occur below the surface of the water as the Big Three simply compete to gain markets, services, and producers.

> We must look at the future of the Big Three to adequately consider disruption. They've had a long, stable run in their current configuration.

Disruption could also occur way above the waterline because the Big Three are in the same business as the giant consulting firms, many of whom are well-capitalized and capable of navigating a merger of some form. The giant, wealthy occupiers of space are also candidates to disrupt the Big Three. Maybe a corporate raider will facilitate the disruption.

It's hard to be a 100-year-old company. Few companies survive that long. Each of the Big Three has been around for more than a century in approximately the same configuration. Maybe that fact alone will be the tipping point for disruption.

ARE YOU READY?

Here are some ideas you could pursue if you perceive that the activity around the Big Three will disrupt your world.

- Read everything you can about Brett White, starting with the article in *The Real Deal*.[9] You could set up a Google Alert on Brett so that, when he makes the news, you'll be able to catch on quickly.

- Each of the Big Three has a robust social media presence. You can pay attention to them through many channels. The leaders occasionally make appearances on national television as well. Check out this clip from Jim Cramer's Mad Money.[10]

- Mike Lipsey has conducted his "Top 25 Commercial Real Estate Brand Survey" for more than twenty years. You can look at the archived reports, free, on his website.[11] It's interesting to note his methodology since he considers several metrics and sources of feedback in his ranking. His winners include landlords and tech companies in addition to brokerage houses. You can see the evolution of the commercial real estate brokerage arena by reading a fifteen-year-old report and comparing it to the most recent one.

- For you fellow old dogs, check out the new office space that CBRE has designed for itself in Singapore. You can find the video on YouTube by searching on "CBRE Singapore's New Workplace360 Office." It's an impressive space—and one small demonstration of how much the commercial real estate brokerage arena has evolved in our lifetimes.

PART THREE

DEMOGRAPHIC EVOLUTION

CHAPTER 8

OLD AGE

Many commercial real estate agents have a different agenda
as they prepare to leave the business.

"Yes, I am sixty-two years old," Rick admitted.
"But, hey, two of the three best years I've ever had have occurred over the past two years. And I'm only working about thirty hours a week." Rick was practically gushing with excitement.

"Sixty-two is the new forty-two, baby!"

As I wander the country talking with agents, I see a lot of faces that look like Rick's. The NAR, CCIM, and SIOR surveys are correct: the average age of a commercial real estate agent in this country is pegged at sixty years old. That seems about right, based on my own experience and small sample size.

Because we've been on an extended upswing, many of these "average age" agents are having years of record earnings. Now, they have no thought of slowing down, much less completely retiring. Many of them are settled in their agencies, their teams, and their marketplaces. They have some valuable relationships, and their style of business (although a little on the old school side of the ledger) still works. It's relatively easy to keep on keeping on.

So, what's the problem?

THE DISRUPTIVE FORCE

Try to imagine being sixty years old (or in that neck of the woods). Your story might look like this:

- You are in relatively good health.

- Your personal life is not very dramatic.

- Your business life is under control.

- Your kids and other family stakeholders are relatively stable.

- You've established an annual budget that keeps you living below your means—you enjoy some nice things and vacations, give some money away, and still put some dollars into savings.

- You have accumulated some wealth—probably not all that you will ever need, but enough to envision retirement.

You are also a child of the Greatest Generation—your parents—who taught you to work hard and gain an education. You've prospered overall, and have a generally optimistic outlook for the future. In fact, AARP reports that 40 percent of this age group is so happy that "I will work until I drop."

Hmm. Doesn't seem very disruptive so far. Let's take a little closer look, though, at your business goals for the next ten years.

Wealth over income. Because you can invest in commercial real estate (you have the money, the relationships, the market knowledge, and the desire), this goal is just as important to you as earning fees. This means:

- You spend as much time looking for deals as making them.

- You spend as much time making your own deals as you do on client transactions.

- You are as sensitive to the needs of your own portfolio as you are to those of your clients.

- You want to self-manage the conflict-of-interest issue—you don't want entanglements with your brokerage platform.

Personal productivity over teambuilding. Because you might be in the last years of your brokerage career, you are less concerned with the evolution of your team than finishing strong personally. This means:

- You are cooperative with your teammates, but you aren't particularly interested in leading your team if it takes a hefty time commitment.

- Mentoring is not nearly as interesting to you as it once was.

- Recruiting is not interesting to you at all.

- Your most important teammate is your personal assistant.

Individual goals over agency goals. Because you have contributed to the company for many years and see yourself with emeritus status, you are less concerned with the profitability of the company and more concerned with the effectiveness of your own practice. This means:

- You want the highest possible split at the lowest threshold of earnings so you can maximize your portion of the commissions you generate.

- You are indifferent to the company's newfangled CRM and don't want to load your thirty-five years of relationships into a public portal.

- You want to attend the minimum number of company meetings, training sessions, and HR briefings.

I can hear all you sixty-somethings out there: "Yeah, that's about right. So what? How are we being disruptive? I cause the least drama of anyone on the floor."

I get it—I'm a sixty-something myself. I didn't say that as a group we are a force for evil. I'm just asking you to think about what the cumulative impact of this mindset will be on the commercial real estate brokerage industry over the next decade.

THE IMPLICATION

You could look at this demographic structure in many ways. Perhaps your office consists of thirty- and forty-year-olds and this just doesn't seem to apply to you. Or perhaps you have five guys over seventy in your office still coming to work every day, and you don't sense any alarm.

You might simply assign it to the "aging of America." The Baby Boomer demographic bubble has been identified for years. Over the next decade, our community will experience the same shifts that are already visible among lawyers, accountants, consultants, and even doctors: more women participants, more diversity, more first-generation Americans.

Here's an easy way to think about this: in many CBRE offices across the country, there is a wall of fame that displays the photographs of the Top Five salespeople (the highest earners) for each year of the past one, two… or five decades. Most of those photos look remarkably similar. The photograph for 2030 is likely to look significantly different, mostly because the sales floor looks significantly different than it did twenty years ago.

By itself, this disruption is probably positive. (Not all disruption is negative. Many of us are extremely thankful that Uber has arrived.) In many ways, diversity alone will make our industry stronger. Maybe we should call it reshaping rather than disruption.

The element that is unique to our community is the expertise that will be leaving the building over the next decade. The 60+ crowd learned the business by hand—we made cold calls in person and wrote notes on business cards. We called the next appointment from a pay phone and started the process of a cold call by warming up the gatekeeper. We calculated mortgage payments and internal rates of return on yellow pads. We earned our salesman skills at the hands of professional trainers. We took clients out to lunch and played golf with them. We saw them in church. We had significant role models within our offices. It seems to me that the success, today, of many of our senior citizens within the community is due to this upbringing.

> The element that is unique to our community is the expertise that will be leaving the building over the next decade.

Perhaps these are merely the musings of an old guy. Maybe the history doesn't matter. Change won't really come very fast, and it won't be attributed to demographics when it does.

On the other hand, I see many new entrants into the industry begging for mentorship, starving for training and unable to identify a role model. I believe *Thrive* has succeeded due to this thirst for guidance. I see the high-split franchises growing (the salesperson keeps 90 percent-plus of the commission, and the agency just charges a low membership fee). I see tremendous focus on email blasts and non-personal communication.

It makes me wonder whether the inevitable march of time will be the change agent, and whether the departure of the Baby Boomers will be as impactful as our arrival.

ARE YOU READY?

Here are some ideas you could pursue if you perceive that the Old Age effect will disrupt your world.

- If you are one of the "average age" agents, make sure you're prepared for the next ten years. You should have a plan, a budget, a portfolio, a will, and tickets for your next trip. Enjoy yourself.

- If you are younger than the average age, my suggestion would be to take time to clearly define your goals over the next ten years. I often ask my coaching clients to "define the lighthouse": While we are out in the open sea, madly bailing water and rowing as fast as we can, could we take a moment to pick out the lighthouse on the horizon so we could paddle in that direction?

  The younger generation is likely to be exposed to more fragmentation, less mentorship, and less long-term perspective than the average-age agents experienced. If this were to be true, it seems like the need to envision the future is even more critical. This younger generation will need mentors and long-term perspective. Where will they come from?

- Confirm the average in your own office. List the agents and their average age. Make another column labeled "Likelihood to last ten more years." Assuming you stayed in the same seat for the next decade, how many chairs around you would change? How do you feel about this prognosis?

- Give this idea a twirl: What is the most significant thing you could learn from the five most important sixty-year-olds in your business environment? Maybe it's time for a good old-fashioned lunch.

CHAPTER 9

NEW AGE

Would a rising star choose to be an agent, or just create the app?

I was milling around at the 2018 CRETech Conference in New York City. More than a thousand people attended, and we were on break between the panel discussions. Some people wandered over to the coffee bar, while the rest of us worked our way through the trade show area.

I already felt a little out of place. I wasn't wearing a hoodie or Allbirds. I had never heard so much tech talk about real estate, and I was trying desperately to write down every new venture-capital phrase I heard. Who knew that the pizza party was such an integral part of the early-stage agenda?

A booth caught my eye, and as I walked toward the booth, the hipster tech dude greeted me. As he explained that he had created a software system that would give a brokerage agency much greater insight into each agent's productivity, I almost glazed over.

"Could you show me?" I asked.

He proceeded to walk me through the system. Although I didn't grasp all of it, I could see that the system had some valuable elements. When I asked how he had learned about the problem he was resolving, he told me he had studied his father's brokerage company.

I asked about his background. "I graduated from business school and then went into software sales in the southwest. Five years later, I earned my MBA and went to Wall Street for a couple of years. Essentially, I was a quant [quantitative analyst]. I came home for a break two years ago and never went back," he explained.

"Why not?" I asked.

"My dad, who's owned his own brokerage company for twenty years—and makes good money as both an agent and the agency owner—showed me how he was struggling to measure the performance of his agents. I fooled with it for a couple of days and then figured out that not only could we solve the problem, we could license the solution to anyone else who had the same problem."

"Did anyone else have the same problem?"

"Everyone did—which is why we're here with a booth. We're the leading solution."

"Are you making any money yet?"

Smirk. "Yup."

THE DISRUPTIVE FORCE

A few months later, I asked one of my more tech-savvy clients if he was familiar with the software.

"Yes. We use it."

"Do you like it?"

"Mostly. They continue to make improvements. It's almost there."

I felt the phantom of disruption brush by me. It's not the software. It's the hipster tech dude.

Let's consider a hypothetical story that starts ten years ago. The successful father/agent would have drawn his smart twenty-two-year-old son into his twenty-year-old brokerage company, first as an agent and then as a future owner. The son would have learned at the foot of the master, and the journeyman would evolve into apprentice and then into craftsman. After twenty years at the firm, the forty-two-year-old son would be the second-generation owner of a forty-year-old brokerage firm. One day, the father calls the son in for an important meeting.

"I appreciate the effort you've invested in the firm, and I'm proud of the contribution our firm has made to our clients, our community, and our team members over the last four decades. It's been a great run. But—if you want to move in a new direction, that's your sole decision. If you want to sell the firm, you can. You own it now, and you have my blessing," the father said.

Let's play out that sell-the-firm scenario as if it were happening today. The agency had average annual gross revenue of about $5 million and generated about $1 million in pre-tax net income. A national brokerage organization agreed to buy the agency for $3 million. The son wanted more, but the national firm hedged since the father (the historical top producer) was retiring immediately, and the purchase agreement called for the son to be paid a guaranteed annual agency-management salary of $175,000 for each of the three years until the purchase price was fully paid out.

In effect, the son sold the firm for three times net earnings after forty years of evolution.

Let's look at a parallel scenario. The son does not join his father out of business school. Instead, he goes to the southwest and then MBA school and then Wall Street. He comes home at age thirty. He develops the software system, tests it on his father's firm, and then begins to license it. He continually improves the software and builds the licensing base up to 500 subscribers, each paying $100 per month. His firm has gross revenues of $600,000 and enjoys an upward trend in subscriptions and client satisfaction. Earlier this year, 275 people attended the user conference, and one-third of them upgraded their account. The son is now thirty-three years old.

He sells his software company to a larger tech firm for $3 million, or five times gross revenue. To the larger firm, the software is in an instant enhancement to their existing platform in the commercial real estate brokerage arena, and they believe they can realize 100 percent return on investment in two years.

"Where's the disruption?" you may ask.

Consider the options in front of the smart son. He can work for twenty years and sell his service business for three times *net* income. Or, he can work for three years and sell his subscription-based software company for five times *gross* income. Of course, he must create something valuable to make the big sale, but if he misses, he can try again. You only have to get it right once. What would you do?

The chart below shows estimated 2018 valuations for both tech companies and CBRE, the largest commercial real estate brokerage agency in the world.

Company	Gross Revenue	Valuation	Comparative Value
Apple	$229B	$878B	3.8x GR
Google	$110B	$720B	6.5x GR
Facebook	$65B	$506B	7.8x GR
Amazon	$178B	$708B	4.0x GR
Redfin[a]	$267M	$1.8B	6.7x GR
Zillow[a]	$1.1B	$8.6B	7.8x GR
CBRE[b]	$21B	$20.2B	1.0x GR

a. Residential real estate tech company
b. Commercial real estate brokerage company

The only conclusion you can draw from this chart is that the new-fangled tech companies that have emerged over the past ten to twenty years are worth four to eight times their top-line revenues, while the biggest commercial real estate brokerage, more than 100 years old, is worth about one time its gross revenue. Do you think this is lost on the rising stars who have an interest in real estate?

There are students sitting in entrepreneurship programs across the country who are acutely attuned to this new formula. We (the old dogs) learned that you manage a tight ship in order to squeeze profit out of the operation. They (the young pups) are learning about eyeballs vs. engagement, and year-over-year growth, and data mining, and revenue multiples.

One top university graduate student told me that their capstone project was to scour the business world for industries that had three qualifications: monopolistic players, limited integration of technology, and lots of iterations (frequent selling events). Those three ingredients essentially set the stage for disruption in the minds of new tech warriors. In other words, find a niche where they've been doing it the same way for a long time and go after the giants. Hmm. Does that sound like an industry you know?

—◦◦◦—

Let's look at this question from another angle. NAIOP is a fifty-year-old international commercial real estate trade organization. On its website, you can find a list of nearly 100 domestic universities that offer an undergraduate or graduate degree (or both) in real estate. The universities offer the courses in a wide variety of formats and often have actively engaged advisory boards. The students have opportunities to participate in local and national case-study competitions, usually focused on the feasibility of a real project on a real site. I'm an alumnus of the University of Florida's undergraduate and graduate degree program, and the sixty-year-old department is stronger than ever. The long trains of alumni are networked together and contribute time, talent, and money to the program. Many of the programs across the country are thriving.

Each program has a different focus but generally offers a menu of courses that include some combination of these topics: development, asset management, master planning, community enrichment, market analysis, valuation, lending, capital markets, global finance, legal issues, municipal regulation—and the list goes on. None that I know of offer a course in brokerage or sales.

Why not?

The reasons are simple to list: The professors are not trained in sales. Brokerage is not considered to be an academic subject. Selling isn't really considered to be a profession. The brokerage houses offer training.

Perhaps the single most impactful reason? *The students don't want to take classes in brokerage.*

You've probably been involved with these university real estate programs as a student, adjunct professor, board member, donor, guest speaker, parent of a student—

> **Students rarely choose to study real estate so they can go into sales.**

you've seen this play out right in front of you. Students rarely choose to study real estate so they can go into sales. They want to be developers. They want to be on Wall Street. They want to be an asset manager for a REIT. Many times, students choose to get an MBA with a real estate concentration when they are twenty-eight years old, just so they can advance more quickly at the bank at which they are already employed.

When I was at the University of Florida, the only honorable thing to do with a real estate degree was to become an appraiser. We took classes that counted for some of the prerequisites to earn an appraisal designation.

Because the bar is so low to become a commercial real estate agent— all you have to do is get a real estate license from your state commission—why would I want to get a degree in sales?

Let's say that there are 100 real estate degree programs (undergraduate plus graduate) at accredited universities in the US. Let's presume that the average number of graduates, annually, from each program is forty. So, the formal real estate education machine turns out 4,000 graduates per year. How many of those graduates choose brokerage?

Based on my extensive travel across the country working with brokerage agencies, I'd say less than 5 percent of the 4,000 graduates choose brokerage as a career path. Maybe two students in a class of forty make that choice. Of the hundreds of agents that you know, how many have degrees in real estate?

Here's another metric that might help specify the number of real estate degree holders who move into brokerage careers. The CCIM designation is available to practitioners who pass four core courses and a small handful of other prerequisites. The CCIM Institute has courted the universities offering real estate programs and offered this proposition: If you qualify for our University Alliance program, we will grant your students (upon graduation) credit for three of our four core courses. This means that a student need take only one of the Institute's four core courses (the course known as CI 103—User Analysis) in order to proceed toward the designation. It's a generous offer because it saves the student at least three weeks of full-time study and several thousand dollars.

I am a CI 103 instructor for the Institute, teaching the course three to four times per year over the past ten years. The typical CI 103 class has twenty to forty students in it. I rarely encounter a student in the CCIM class who is taking advantage of the three-course-waiver opportunity. In other words, few students with real estate degrees take advantage of the Institute offer. Unless they want to go into brokerage, why would they?

To be fair, let's take a broader look at this "university" issue. I once had a long conversation with the dean of the business school at a major university. The dean was relatively new to his position, and he was marveling at the growth of the real estate department in his college. Many donors had stepped forward to assist the program, and although the department was less than ten years old, it already had a significant annual conference and a growing advisory board.

Then the dean made an interesting comment. "I'm not sure we should be teaching real estate to our students."

The dean's case was that real estate education at the university level was a choice too narrow for the student. He offered that if a student wanted to learn more about real estate, after graduation, there were many excellent industry-based sources for that education. "Would a student be better off studying psychology or political science or communication or literature at the university—subjects we are really good at—and then with that broader background, go learn about real estate in the industry?"

I agreed. I told him, "I've found that once you leave the university, it is really hard to create an immersive learning environment in the subjects you've listed. I agree that those subjects would create a more well-rounded future agent."

If my premise is correct, you don't have a degree in real estate. You have degrees in finance or art history or biology or religious studies. Perhaps you've never used your degree in your professional career. Somehow, you found your way into the brokerage arena. The dean's case is that you've been exposed to a bigger picture, which is valuable to your status as a human, and then found another source to learn what you needed to know to be successful as an agent.

So, if the smart, young whippersnappers don't want to become commercial real estate agents, where does that leave us?

THE IMPLICATION

The implication is clear: Smart young people can earn more money, faster, by developing technology applications for commercial real estate than they can by working as a commercial agent. The start-up period for a commercial agent is notoriously slow: Many agents do not crack the $100,000 threshold until at least three years of work. If you are going to starve for three years, why not do it as a software developer where the potential payoff is much, much greater?

Even if they fail to deliver the big payday, young entrepreneurs may end up with small businesses that generate monthly income (a nice safety feature when planning to go into brokerage). Or the knowledge they will gain building their own app makes them a much stronger candidate for employment in the IT departments of the big brokerage firms that are now going to CRETech Conferences and hanging out with venture capitalists.

In the 2018 CRETech Conference, there was general agreement among all the panelists from the big brokerage firms: They would much rather buy applications than develop them. "We'll only develop them if we can't find a solution to buy," one panelist said to nods all around.

Many smart young people are interested in real estate from a traditional perspective. These students demonstrate that choice by pursuing real estate degrees but then rarely choosing brokerage as a path. Regardless of whether today's students are not choosing brokerage even as they study real estate (not a new phenomenon) or are pulled toward real-estate-related technology (a new phenomenon), the commercial real estate brokerage industry is not generating a compelling value proposition for the next generation.

This is not shocking news. Many trade organizations have held entire symposiums on "recruiting" strategies. The questions are many, and the answers are few. A common refrain is that we must create meaningful pathways into the brokerage arena that include effective training and financial support along the way.

Based on my travels, I'd say the typical onboarding program for new agents looks something like this: Start as a researcher or analyst, possibly as the low man on a brokerage team. You're paid an entry-level salary, usually by the company, but sometimes with partial compensation support by the brokers on the team. After a year or so, you are invited to become a junior agent and given a draw of, say, $3,000 per month for up to a year. (*Draw* is prepaid commission. If the agent earns a commission, the current draw balance is deducted from the commission before any money flows to the agent. Accordingly, most first-year agents rarely earn more than their draw. If the draw balance were large at the end of the year—say, $25,000—the agent and the firm have hard decisions to make. The firm is concerned about whether it will ever recover the loan it has made, and the agent wonders whether he will ever pay off the loan.)

Assuming the agent survives, both the junior agent and the agency assume that by the end of this second year, there will be a low (or preferably, zero) draw balance. The agent has earned low wages for these first two years. In the third year with the company, the agent will be on full commission, without the safety net of a draw. The challenge is to find a niche on the brokerage team that gives the young agent a clear shot at significant earnings—let's say $100,000 in commissions that flow to him. The issue of whether the agent has been appropriately trained to command that value in the marketplace is decidedly fuzzy.

If this is an accurate depiction of our value proposition to new agents, would you advise your child to pursue it?

The biggest brokerages are addressing this challenge in earnest. Their "head of global learning and training" has a lot more traction in the organization now, and more resources are being directed toward the new agents. These companies are making aggressive use of internal and external resources. But if my estimate is true that the Big Three brokerage companies account for only 8 percent of the agents in the industry, is this enough? What is the typical experience of the average agent who is not associated with the Big Three?

What is the ideal entry program? How far are we from that ideal?

ARE YOU READY?

Here are some ideas you could pursue if you perceive that the New Age effect will disrupt your world.

- Attend a CRETech Conference. (CRETech is a specific brand; many technology conferences are offered by many brands each year.)

Several thousand people participate in these conferences. Even if you are one of the "average age" agents and don't plan to integrate much new technology in your practice, you should treat yourself to the whole new language that is evolving.

- While you are at the conference, keep your eyes open for an opportunity to invest in *optech* (software that makes agencies perform effectively in the areas of analysis, market data, marketing materials, etc.) or *proptech* (software that makes real estate perform more effectively in the areas of security, energy efficiency, lifecycle analysis, etc.). Even if you merely evaluate an opportunity, you will learn totally new ideas.

- If you have an acute interest in the evolution of smart young people into commercial real estate technologists, check out the Proptech Techstars Accelerator hosted by Colliers International. This is the direct merger of early-stage tech companies seeking funding for their software applications in the commercial real estate arena. In other words, Colliers is actively seeking to draw entrepreneurs into the world of tech solutions for our arena. More than 800 people participated, live, in the 2018 Demo Day in Toronto. The 2019 event is shaping up like this: 300 applications for the program, drawn from 20,000 applicants, qualified to be coached by 150 mentors prior to Demo Day.

- Find a way to get closer to a university real estate program. At the least, get close enough to observe the job selection/hiring process. What are these students seeking, and what are the employers offering? Try hiring one of these scholars yourself. How does your value proposition compare to their other offers?

CONCLUSION

After many days of trying to communicate my thoughts in writing, it was time to relax. My wife and I rewarded ourselves with a stay at a luxury resort, and it seemed to me that a jaunt to the day spa was completely justified. I had visions of a steam bath, a dip in the pool, and then one of those exotic teas on the veranda. I could feel the plush bathrobe and soft slippers enfolding me, and I was leaning in. Maybe I would even sign up for an expensive essential-oil massage on the next day.

When I arrived at the spa, the "facilitator" greeted me. Hmm. I quickly discovered that the spa of my memory had changed. A lot. I was shown through the facility in which I could float in a sensory deprivation pod. (Would I like meditative music or the birds of the equator as my sound guide?) I could take a spinning class with a remote instructor or work with a virtual-reality guide that would take me on a tour of the local cuisine without leaving the spa.

"Um, this seems a lot different than the last time I was here."

"Yes, sir. We've really focused on experiential interaction. We still offer some of the 'traditional services,' as we call them, but we encourage our guests to try something new."

I later ran into the hotel manager. She told me that operating the spa had become so costly—primarily due to the wages of highly specialized service providers—that it was caught in a downward spiral. The operating costs were high, so the prices to the guests were high, and the spa was drifting from profit to loss.

"We were losing money, big time. But when we really dug into the experiences that our guests enjoyed most while they are here, we discovered we could use the spa to enhance those experiences."

"Really? Could you give me an example?"

"Sure. Floating in a saline pod takes the same hour that a massage does. The cost of us offering the service and the price that the guest pays is a fraction of a massage, partly because our attendant only spends about five minutes with the guest prior to launching the float session. The magic is that the guests rate the floating experience on par with a massage. On the first day, the adventurous spouse tries out the pod, and then both return on the second day. They feel good because their total expenditure for two people is less than the cost of one massage for one person, and we make a reasonably good profit."

Ahh. Our old friend Creative Destruction had visited without even letting me know. The services offered by the spa were different, the type of staff and the cost of that staff was different, and the guest experience was totally unexpected.

Floating in a sensory deprivation pod was unlike anything I had ever experienced, and I took an hour-long spinning class—as a solo student wearing a Bluetooth headset and heart rate monitor strapped to my chest. I ranked #1,970 out of the 4,533 spinners that had participated that month, but I was #3 in my age group. Yeah, I've still got it.

—◆—

Welcome to what the future is going to feel like. You will encounter creative destruction so frequently you'll no longer be shocked when it occurs. You may marvel at the changes for a while, but you'll soon become so accustomed to the new and improved value proposition that you'll come to expect it.

I used to interview all my Uber drivers about their experiences and how the app works from their perspective and whether they were also participating in Uber Eats. Now, I just talk about the weather with my drivers.

This is the experience that we will share with our clients and prospects in the days to come. It is already starting to occur, and the "early-warning signals" are all around us.

In the "Introduction," I asked how you felt about the creative destruction of our industry. Are you resistant to change? Are you resistant because you like things the way they are? Or is it because you had to learn so much to get to this point that learning a new way seems too much to handle?

Perhaps you look forward to the new order of business. You agree with Alan Kay's vision that the best way to predict the future is to invent it. From your perspective, the future is the best thing that could happen to us.

Maybe you are in the middle—you just want to avoid being the crab. You know—the crab that is initially placed in warm water and never reacts until the water starts to boil. You are not an early adopter, but you will eventually adapt.

Regardless of your perspective, I have tried to think out in front of us. I've identified forces that seem particularly capable of disrupting our industry. I've researched those forces and formed my own conclusions, and I have exposed those ideas to hundreds of agents through focus group sessions. The results are in—disruption is coming.

So, if disruption is coming, how can we prepare? How will we adapt? The premise of the book is that you can be aware of these forces, watch for their manifestations, and become more informed as a first step in preparation. Through the nine chapters describing these sources of disruption, I've offered anecdotes, information, statistics, and implications you can consider.

I've listed more than thirty-five activities you could undertake to sharpen your senses.

To some degree, you can measure your receptivity to the coming disruption by what you do now. If you are compelled by the information in this book, you will find yourself touring an Amazon warehouse, or hiring a gig worker, or listing a property on Ten-X. Maybe you'll attend a CRETech Conference, and then find yourself investing in a start-up proptech company. Perhaps you'll find the market leader for one of the consulting companies and have lunch with her.

If not, it is OK. Maybe you'll live comfortably in the idea that we've probably overestimated the amount of change that will happen in a year. Or perhaps you can stay relevant for the last two to three years of your career as you always planned. You might respond with a "let's see how it goes" philosophy.

—⁕—

The undergraduate student bounced up to me and showed me the certification she had earned over the weekend. As a result of spending the better part of three days in a boot camp to learn how to use ARGUS (a complex modeling program used to discount future cash flows into a current value), the student could now show future employers that she was a functional user of this state-of-the-art spreadsheet program. It is a significant accomplishment, and it distinguishes one student from another.

"Nicely done. Was it as hard as you thought it would be?"

"Yes! There is an incredible number of fields that you must enter to ultimately create a price that you would offer for the property."

"What kind of data did you enter in those fields?"

"Oh, estimates about future vacancy and rent and escalations and tenant improvement expenses."

"I see. Hmm. Would it be fair to say that you had to make a lot of assumptions about the future?"

"Absolutely!"

I started to say something dismissive, like "Well, then we can be certain that the exact combination of conditions that you predicted *won't* come true. The one thing we do know is that your estimate of current value is flawed." My fatherly sense kicked in just in time—what was the benefit in diminishing her joy at her accomplishment?

Writing a book about the future, complete with a full set of assumptions, is a lot like working all weekend on an ARGUS run—but being old enough to know that this vision is certain not to come true. No one has enough information and vision and judgment to accurately predict the future. So, what's the use in working on an ARGUS run? Why even contemplate what the future might look like?

Because the future is being created every day. Disruption is the remnant piece of the puzzle—it occurs because one person, and then another, and then another sees just a glimpse of the future. What if we did it this way instead? I wonder, if we tried this path, whether we would get different results; how could I eliminate this one factor that is so painful to my progress?

—⁓—

The small town of Parkfield, California, lies inland about halfway between San Francisco and Los Angeles in Monterey County. You'll have to look for it carefully as you turn north from Cholame on State Route 41—it has a population of only eighteen people (when last surveyed in 2007). What makes Parkfield remarkable, though, is its location along the San Andreas Fault at the intersection between the North American Plate and the Pacific Plate. Since it has experienced half a dozen earthquakes over the past 170 years that have registered a magnitude of 6.0 or greater on the Richter scale, Parkfield proudly proclaims itself as the Earthquake Capital of the World. Twenty years ago, a team of US government scientific agencies bored a two-mile hole into the fault line near Parkfield for the purpose of getting a better look at the epicenter and enhancing the team's ability to predict, or at least warn of, a major earthquake. No wonder that the Parkfield Café has a unique invitation posted near the front door: *Be Here When It Happens.*

The scientists have learned all kinds of interesting things about plate tectonics, including something called *aseismic creep.* In Parkfield, you can see houses that have twisted on their foundations and streets that have essentially torn apart. This is the result of the plates slipping, or creeping, apart. It's a daily reminder that the plates are moving, and an earthquake is coming. Hopefully, the scientists will be able to give us a few minutes to prepare.

The Parkfield project is symbolic of an early-warning system. The movements of the earth that are being measured way down in that two-mile hole are the small insights that scientists gain as the earth evolves. They can literally "feel the earth move under my feet," as the song says.

Being more sensitive to the presence of these small insights into our future might be the best way to prepare for that future. Our industry is positioned between two tectonic plates—the past and the future—and we can feel the tremors of the coming disruption. We have a lot better chance of adapting to our future if we watch for and analyze the early warning signs. Hopefully, we're slightly more prepared for our future as a result of examining and discussing the ideas in this book.

I invite you to join the watch party and add your ideas to the conversation. On the next page, I've provided some discussion questions to jumpstart this process.

STUDY GROUP
DISCUSSION QUESTIONS

In the "Conclusion," I urged you to examine and discuss the ideas in this book as a way of preparing for the future. To that end, I've provided some questions below that may jumpstart this discussion for your group.

INTRODUCTION

a. When you think about "disruption," what is the first scenario that comes to mind?

b. How do you feel about the scenario you've recalled? Are you better or worse off because of the disruption?

c. Envision being in the role that you now have at a point ten years from now. Would you say that the role will be mildly, moderately, or significantly different than it is now? Why?

d. As you scroll through the Contents listing near the beginning of the book, which of the nine forces do you think will be most disruptive in your environment?

PART ONE—CLIENT EVOLUTION

a. To what degree have you used a professional to guide your travel choices? How does that experience relate to your role as a professional advisor?

b. The most tech-savvy client I deal with is: _____. How has this client's savviness changed the services you provide?

c. The most tech-savvy competitor I have is: _____. What benefit is gained by this savviness?

d. How well stated is your personal value proposition? If you decided to put your value proposition into your email signature block, and you limited yourself to twelve words, what would it say?

e. If you were to post a job (seeking someone to complete a task for you) on Upwork, what would it be? If you were to register as a freelancer on Upwork, what service would you offer? Based on the other freelancers who offer a similar service, what hourly rate would you charge?

PART TWO—PLAYGROUND OF THE GIANTS

a. What interaction, related to commercial real estate, have you had with one of the large consulting firms? Which consulting firms are used by your clients?

b. If you were forced to place one of your listings on the Ten-X platform, which one would it be? Why did you choose this property?

c. What is the most remarkable aspect of the services offered by Amazon that you use?

d. Complete this sentence: It won't surprise me to find that Amazon...

e. In terms of comparing the performance of the three largest brokers (CBRE, JLL, and Cushman & Wakefield) to the rest of the brokerage community in your arena, how close is the ratio I've estimated (8 percent of the sales force/50 percent of the commissions)?

f. If you were selected as the chairman of CBRE, what is the first initiative you would undertake?

PART THREE—DEMOGRAPHIC EVOLUTION

a. If there is a generation gap in your firm, how do the players on either side of the gap differ from each other? To what degree are they the same?

b. To what degree is your firm dependent on Baby Boomers (born prior to 1964) for production? How will this change over the next ten years?

c. To what degree do you compete with other agents who are Baby Boomers? What, if any, is the primary benefit they offer to their customers?

d. If you wanted to recruit a student currently enrolled in a graduate-level real estate program, which three programs would be your first choices? What attributes would you be seeking in these young candidates for your firm?

e. If you wanted to invest in a software company with a commercial real estate focus, where would you look to find opportunities?

CONCLUSION

a. In general, how adaptable is your firm to change?

b. If you were seeking an early-warning system for changes about to occur in the commercial real estate brokerage industry, where might you look?

c. What action will you undertake first, as a result of digesting the ideas in this book?

END NOTES

Introduction

1. Jie Zong, Jeanne Batalova, and Micayla Burrows, *Frequently Requested Statistics on Immigrants and Immigration in the United States* (Spotlight, Migration Policy Institute, March 14, 2019), accessed December 1, 2019, https://www.migrationpolicy.org/article/ frequently-requested-statistics-immigrants-and-immigration-united-states.

Chapter 1

2. Doug Gollan, Travel Contributor, "In the Land of Travel Agents, the Tables Have Turned," *Forbes* (August 19, 2018), accessed December 1, 2019, https://www.forbes.com/sites/douggollan/2018/08/19/ in-the-land-of-travel-agents-the-tables-have-turned/#16353c0d5872.

Chapter 3

3. "Metcalfe's Law," *Techopedia*, accessed December 1, 2019, https://www. techopedia.com/definition/29066/metcalfes-law.

4. "Doc Searls." *Wikipedia*, accessed December 1, 2019, https://en.wikipedia.org/ wiki/Doc_Searls.

5. Doc Searls Weblog (multiple posts), accessed December 1, 2019, https://blogs. harvard.edu/doc/.

Chapter 6

6. "Tour an Amazon Fulfillment Center," *The Amazon blog: Day One*, accessed December 1, 2019, https://www.aboutamazon.com/amazon-fulfillment-center-tours/.

7. *Amazon HQ2 RFP*, accessed December 1, 2019, https://images-na.ssl-images-amazon.com/images/G/01/Anything/test/images/usa/RFP_3._V516043504_.pdf.

8. Document Cloud home page, accessed December 1, 2019, https://www.documentcloud.org/.

Chapter 7

9. Adam Piore, "Brett White's War," *The Real Deal* (September 2015), accessed December 1, 2019, https://therealdeal.com/issues_articles/brett-whites-war/.

10. "CBRE Group CEO: Real Estate Expansion/Mad Money/CNBC" *YouTube* video (May 16, 2018), accessed December 1, 2019, https://www.youtube.com/watch?v=7KbBro64YLI.

11. Lipsey Company. *Lipsey's 2019 Top 25 Brand Survey*, accessed December 1, 2019, https://lipseyco.com/brand-survey/.

ACKNOWLEDGMENTS

Any book gets written by a team. I'm lucky to have so many talented team members. From the beginning of this quest, Jim Spaeth has been an encouraging, insightful listener and reader. Many other early readers, including Ed Hanley, Tanner Milne, Beau Beery, and Michael Hefferon have offered valuable contributions.

Sam Katz and Jack Partain were my researchers, and their hard work enabled me to reach much farther than I would have on my own. Dave Walker, Peter Barnett, Bill Moss, Justin Latorre, Trent Scott, and Mark Thompson offered insights into their corners of the commercial real estate arena that were fundamental in shaping my thinking.

My writing coach, Wally Bock, returned to the team for the second book and was a constant source of guidance, truth-telling, and encouragement. When you are on the same page as your coach, the writing process is more challenging and more creative. Thank you, Wally.

Lynette Smith also returned to the team as an editor and used her usual sharp-eyed judgment to make the book more readable. Elena Reznikova helped me think through the design of the book cover.

The most cherished players on my team are my immediate family members. My brother and his wife, Tom and Bonnie Strickland, provided support in many ways, including enabling me to write in a quiet, beautiful nest. My daughter, Casey, and my son, Hunter, were readers and detail-handlers throughout the process. My father,

Robert K. Strickland, has always been an inspiration to me and offered valuable ideas for this book.

My wife of forty years, Eileen, is truly my partner. She was subjected to so many dinner discussions about my ideas and progress that she is essentially a co-author. Thank you, Eileen. I could not have done it without you.

ABOUT THE AUTHOR

H. Blaine Strickland is the personal coach to several of the country's top-producing commercial real estate agents and brokerage firms. His tremendous depth of experience as a broker, manager, owner, developer, syndicator, and consultant over a forty-year career in the commercial real estate arena enable him to provide a broad perspective and deep expertise to his clients.

Along this lifetime journey in the commercial real estate arena, Blaine has also become a professional educator and speaker. He has instructed real estate students at the undergraduate, graduate, and professional levels, and he is frequently called upon to present his ideas at trade association forums across the country.

To learn more about Blaine or to engage him as a speaker, please visit HBS-Resources.com.